"What an incredible resc...
of work and the detail that went into this book. A great window on baseball's lexicon from days of yore – to the game today. This book won't be far from my side next season."

– Dan Dickerson, Voice of the Detroit Tigers

"The Baseball Thesaurus is an interesting read for casual and serious fans alike. It's entertaining, informative, and full of anecdotes I had never come across before."

– Dan Shulman, ESPN

"For fans old and new, Jesse Goldberg-Strassler's thesaurus is a romp. On first glance, it's a primer on baseball's peculiar taxonomy and traditions, but open any page and you'll find lots more, including amusing anecdotes and witty wordplay from the game's great characters. Goldberg-Strassler has built a dugout in which Al Capone, James Earl Jones, and George Carlin lounge happily alongside Dizzy Dean, Cool Papa Bell, and Zoilo Versalles. A lollygagger's delight!"

– John Lott, baseball writer, *National Post*, Toronto

"Baseball has always enjoyed its own unique language. Now we've got a book to prove it. Jesse Golberg-Strassler provides a fascinating read for those new to the game, as well as an education for life-long baseball fans."

– Dave Raymond, former Voice of the Houston Astros

"The Baseball Thesaurus is a must-read whether you are a rabid baseball fanatic who pores through box scores 24/7...or just a casual fan. I can't wait to use some of the nuggets and anecdotes during my broadcasts."

– Kenny Albert, FOX Sports

The Baseball Thesaurus

Jesse Goldberg-Strassler

To Luke,
Here's to some terrific seasons (and many strikeouts)!
Sincerely,
Jesse Goldberg-Strassler

August Publications
Middleton, WI

The Baseball Thesaurus

Lineup Books / August Publications
3543 John Muir Dr.
Middleton, WI 53562
608.836.3730
augustpublications.com

First edition published 2013

ISBN 978-1-938532-02-3

9 8 7 6 5 4 3 2 1

Designer (cover): Funnel Design, Lin Wilson.

Image of Mel Allen courtesy of National Baseball Hall of Fame Library, Cooperstown, NY.

FOREWORD

By Peter Morris

Baseball is often said to be the writer's game. Why? Because it's a sport in which words matter in a way that they don't in its rivals.

Watch a football game and I guarantee you before the color commentator tells you that one of the coaches has "dialed up" a play. Why do they have to dial up plays, you may ask? Couldn't they get a better plan that that? But if you ask a football fan for an explanation, don't expect more than a blank stare in response.

Soon you'll also hear one of the announcers explain that the defensive linemen will be "pinning back their ears" to rush the quarterback. Why do they do that, you may wonder? Does it make them more aerodynamic? Nope, once again it's one of those clichés that football insiders repeat without thinking about.

Similarly, football announcers endlessly tell you that one of the teams "has really come to play" (presumably making the other team's appearance an illusion) and that the middle linebacker is the "heart and soul" of the team, and so on and so forth. Some seem willing to give up language altogether, with Terry Bradshaw often bellowing to no apparent purpose and onetime Monday Night Football announcer Don Meredith occasionally breaking into song.

Baseball is different.

Of course the national pastime has its clichés and even had its Dizzy Dean, whose use of words such as "slud" and "ain't" so distressed English teachers that they petitioned for his removal from the airwaves. Nevertheless, baseball announcers – even Dean – care about the precise use of language and so do baseball fans. Baseball's measured pace forces both analysts and observers to search for *le mot juste* and then to reflect on why a particular word suits that occasion. Mindless repetition of the same stock phrase, in particular, cannot be reconciled with the game's lyrical bent.

This fascination with the endless variations of language is what makes Jesse Goldberg-Strassler's *The Baseball Thesaurus* such a treat. A touchdown is always a touchdown and a goal is just a goal, but as Goldberg-Strassler shows, every baseball term has multiple synonyms. A batter may be a biffer or a swatster or a bludgeon wielder or twenty other possibilities, ranging from the banal to the bizarre.

Best of all, there are no end of subtle nuances that distinguish the various options: a "bad-ball hitter" is one who is adept at hitting pitches outside the strike zone, while a "mistake hitter" feasts upon poor offerings and a "human rain delay" takes too much time between pitches. Even within the distinctions there are distinctions, so that a patient "surveyor" of pitches may be a "camera eye" if his at bats often result in walks, but a "window-shopper" if the umpire frequently calls him out on strikes.

The result is a rich and delightful work that pays fitting tribute to baseball's love affair with language. Broadcasters will immediately recognize *The Baseball Thesaurus* as an essential tool of the trade – indeed, Goldberg-Strassler is a broadcaster himself and wrote the book because he knew how valuable it will be. Fan may appreciate it even more, because it will give them no end of enjoyable browsing.

Best of all, it may save them from having to listen to their favorite team's announcer repeating the same trite phrases.

Peter Morris *first came to prominence by winning the first World Scrabble Championship in 1991 and has gained enduring fame through immense contributions in the field of baseball research and literature. His first book,* Baseball Fever, *provided a detailed look at Michigan baseball from its beginnings up to the 1870s, while his second book, the acclaimed two-volume* Game of Inches, *is the definitive canon on the origins of every aspect of the national pastime. His most recent work is* Catcher: How the Man Behind the Plate Became an American Folk Hero. *Morris resides in East Lansing, Michigan.*

Introduction

Who is this thesaurus for?

It's for the media linguist whose job relies upon baseball jargon, the radio listener, the blog reader, the talk-show caller, the minor-league diehard, the Strat-O-Matic connoisseur, the seventh-inning stretcher, the stereotype breaker, the crank, the postgame fireworks enthusiast, the t-ball coach, the seamhead, the baseball Annie, the hot-stove moper, the bandwagoner, the purist, the casual rooter who enjoys a quick tidbit and has no need to attend both games of a doubleheader, and the fan who takes pride in scoring the game and teaching the tradition to others.

There are more different types of baseball fans than there are slang names for fans. Everyone enjoys the game in their own way for their own reasons, whether emotional, mathematical, or anecdotal.

I fall on the anecdotal side. I love the stories of the game, and I love the language used to tell those stories.

Growing up in Maryland, my evenings were accompanied by the masterfully evocative voices of Chuck Thompson and Jon Miller. In 2005, fresh out of Ithaca College, I entered the field of minor-league baseball broadcasting – and soon learned how easy it was to slip into unimaginative ruts. I used the same words throughout each game. Home runs were consistently "drilled." Runners perpetually "cruised" into second base.

Motivated to improve, I brainstormed an abundance of ways to describe a batter hitting the ball, a baserunner running the bases, a pitcher releasing his next pitch, and a fielder making a defensive play. Many a broadcaster before me must have enjoyed the same exercise; imagine stealing a glance over the shoulder of an Ernie Harwell or Vin Scully as he touches pen to paper to create his own brainstormed lists.

After several seasons passed, I shared my work with Jon Chelesnik, who posted it on his Sportscasters Talent Agency of America forums. A conversation in early 2010 with fellow broadcaster Joe Davis spurred the creation of something larger, a thesaurus for the world of baseball.

The project received the blessing of Paul Dickson and Skip McAfee, who included a thesaurus in their second edition of the authoritative and indispensable **The Dickson Baseball Dictionary** in 1999. (They excluded the section when the third edition was published in 2009.) Coaches, players, and broadcasters all assisted in compiling a diverse array of baseball vocabulary and description, with Spanish terms supplied by Antonio Caceres.

In early 2011, obstacles arose and the baseball thesaurus nearly transformed into something else entirely. *National Post* baseball writer John Lott connected me with pitcher/bestselling author Dirk Hayhurst, who suggested that I go inside the clubhouse and grab more cutting player jargon. As an example:

Wetting the bed: When a pitcher falls apart on the mound. *Ex.: "Hayhurst wet the bed in his outing against the Dodgers."*

There's a book there somewhere, without a doubt, but it never worked out. I did chase after the concept for a while, though. Here, for your enjoyment, are Toronto Blue Jays farmhand Mark Sobolewski's contributions:

Gas Can: A reliever who comes into a game and immediately kills any chance his team had to win. He's the opposite of a firefighter; he pours gasoline on the blaze.
Ex.: "We're bringing in the gas can to pitch the 6th? That's it for this game."

Harry Potter: An unassuming, unimposing pitcher who has mediocre stuff, but still manages to frustrate hitters and record outs. Bonus points for wearing glasses.
Ex.: "How am I 0-for-3 against Harry Potter out there?"

Pizza Man: A player, often roundly disliked, who looks entirely out of place and must have only come to the baseball stadium in order to deliver a pizza.
Ex.: "Did you see that pizza man taking batting practice?"

In the end, with thanks to Kevin Reichard and August Publications (and apologies to Dirk and Mark), the thesaurus remained intact. Here it is for your pleasure, whether you're a Harry Potter or a Houdini, a Pizza Man or a Picasso.

– Jesse Goldberg-Strassler

Acknowledgments

Hearty thanks are owed to Kevin Reichard, Paul Dickson and Skip McAfee, Shayna Skolnik, Steve Stewart, Jerry Coleman, Dave Raymond, Jim Tocco, Patrick Day, Dan Dickerson, Joe Davis, Jon Chelesnik, Antonio Caceres, Sal Fasano, John Tamargo Jr., Drew Stein, Dirk Hayhurst, John Lott, Neil Smith, Adam Korn, Sean Ochinko, Ben Chiswick, Nick Devlin, Larry Dumeney, Tom Gauthier, Brad Golder, Tom Nichols, Rosalie Petrouske, and Owen Serey. Ari and Dina are looking for their names here, too, and so I might as well oblige them.

For my father

Members of the 1937 All-Star Game played on July 7 in Washington, D.C. Left to right: Lou Gehrig, Joe Cronin, Bill Dickey, Joe DiMaggio, Charlie Gehringer, Jimmie Foxx, and Hank Greenberg.
(Courtesy Library of Congress, LC-DIG-hec-22989.)

All-Star Game
n. Midsummer Classic (or midsummer classic), showcase of stars, Summer Classic; summer showcase; SPANISH juego de estrella

• The first Major League Baseball All-Star Game was held July 6, 1933, at Comiskey Park, home of the White Sox. The location was no accident; *Chicago Tribune* sports editor Arch Ward organized the exhibition as part of the

World's Fair in Chicago. (In 1962, the Arch Ward Trophy was created to honor the game's Most Valuable Player.) With 47,595 in attendance, Babe Ruth homered to spearhead a 4-2 American League victory. According to *Baseball Uniforms of the 20th Century*, the National League opened up its wallet to clad its players in identical uniforms while the AL squad suited up in their home jerseys and enjoyed pizza after the game with the money they'd saved.

• Only six pitchers were used in the first All-Star Game, three by each team. Each team boasted an 18-man roster, nine starters and nine reserves. In contrast, there were 20 pitchers and 43 total All-Stars – including injured players and their replacements – on the 2011 American League squad. (Note that there were only eight teams in the AL in 1933 compared to double that in modern baseball.)

• From 1935 through 1946, the All-Star rosters were determined solely by managers. In the first year of this process, Detroit Tigers first baseman Hank Greenberg was snubbed by his own manager, Mickey Cochrane, despite leading the league at the All-Star Break with an astounding 103 RBI.

• From *Bill Mazer's Amazin' Baseball Book*, "The midsummer classic of 1945 was never played. The country and 'The Game' were so engulfed by the Second World War that the game was canceled. Instead, Baseball Commissioner Happy Chandler scheduled exhibition contests played by major-league teams against minor-league clubs, military clubs (often laced with major-league stars), and college teams. The proceeds were diverted to the war effort."

• A second All-Star Game was added in 1959 in order to raise money for the players' pensions. In 1963, concerned that the game's appeal was being diluted, the players went back to playing just one All-Star Game per summer.

• In 2003, citing widespread disinterest in the All-Star Game, Major League Baseball added the debatable incentive of World Series home-field advantage for the victorious league.

"I'd rather go fishing for three days."
– Hall of Fame manager Dorrel "Whitey" Herzog (1973-1990)

artificial turf
n. artificial grass, artificial surface, blanket, carpet, plastic, rug, synthetic field, synthetic surface, turf, turface; SPECIFIC AstroTurf (or Astroturf), FieldTurf; SPANISH grama artificial

"Don't get me wrong: I have nothing good to say about artificial turf. But the baseball of the 1970s, which was derived in part from the artificial turf that was then so popular, was a wonderful brand of baseball. On the field at one time you might have a player who was capable of hitting .350 or better, a baserunner who was capable of stealing 80 or more bases, a hitter who was capable of hitting 35 or 40 homers, and a 20-game winner who could strike out 250 or 300 batters."
– Bill James, *The New Bill James Historical Baseball Abstract*

• The Houston Astrodome opened in 1965 with real grass, but the stadium's ceiling panels restricted the necessary sunlight and caused the Astros to play on a surface of painted dirt. AstroTurf replaced the grass for 1966, officially introducing artificial turf to baseball. By the

1970s, the new facilities in Pittsburgh, Philadelphia, St. Louis, and Cincinnati (denigrated as "cookie-cutter stadiums" for their many similarities) also featured artificial turf.

• There are currently two teams in the Major Leagues who play their home games on artificial turf: the Tampa Bay Rays play on AstroTurf at Tropicana Field, while the Toronto Blue Jays play on FieldTurf at Rogers Centre (formerly SkyDome).

"How can you hit inside a dome when you grew up listening to your mother tell you not to play ball inside the house?"

– outfielder Kurt Bevacqua (1971-1985), *It's Anybody's Ballgame*

at-bat

n. AB, attempt, crack, cut, go, lick, try, turn, up; SPANISH turno

• An official at-bat is any plate appearance that does not end in a walk, hit batsman, catcher's interference, sacrifice bunt, or sacrifice fly.

• An *at-bat* is also used to describe the entirety of a half-inning of offense. (See *inning* for more synonyms.)

• scheduled to bat next

n. in the slot, in the on-deck circle, on deck, to follow, up next, waiting in the wings

• scheduled to bat in two hitters

n. in the hold (the original phrase, meaning below deck on a ship), in the hole (a corrupted form of the original)

"Nothing's more exciting than knowing you've got four at-bats every day. There's nothing better in life than that. I don't have kids. I don't have hobbies. This is what I do – I hit."

– first baseman Mo Vaughn (1991-2003), *Sports Illustrated;* July 1, 1996

B

At one point the National Bureau of Standards tested baseballs for quality. Edward B. Eynon (left), Secretary of the Washington Baseball Club, and Dr. Hugh L. Dryden, Chief of the Mechanics and Sound Division, who designed the unique machine used in the tests, are discussing the first ball to be hit by the Government Fence Buster, taken February 1938.
(Courtesy Library of Congress, LC-H22-D- 3301.)

ballpark
n. see *baseball field*

balls and strikes
n. There is no direct synonym for either "ball," a pitch thrown outside of the strike zone, or "strike," a pitch taken inside the strike zone, fouled off by the batter, or swung at and missed.

• The "count" is the amount of balls and strikes on the current batter. Four balls grant the batter a walk while three strikes equal a strikeout, nice and simple…although, due to player and umpire inattention, the Mets' Lenny Randle managed to line a triple against the Phillies on a 4-and-2 pitch on May 5, 1978, while the snoozing 2011 Seattle Mariners issued walks on just three balls to a willing Cameron Maybin on July 2 and an unknowing Bobby Abreu on July 10. Even more costly, Maybin scored the only run in a 1-0 San Diego victory.

• The number of balls is provided before the number of strikes. If there are no balls and one strike, the count is "0-and-1" or "nothing and 1." The next pitch is considered "the 0-1 pitch," "the one-strike pitch," or "the strike-one pitch." Likewise, a count of one ball and no strikes would make the next pitch "the 1-0," "the one-ball pitch," or "the ball-one pitch."

• An "even" count occurs when there are the same number of balls as strikes. The next pitch is the "break-even."

• A "hitter's count" has more balls than strikes, giving the hitter the advantage. The 1-0, 2-0, 2-1, and 3-1 counts are hitter's counts, putting the pitcher "in a hole." In a hitter's count, the hitter is considered "ahead in the count" while the pitcher is "behind in the count."

• A "pitcher's count" occurs when there are more strikes than balls, giving the pitcher the advantage. The 0-1, 0-2, and 1-2 counts are pitcher's counts, putting the batter "in a hole." In a pitcher's count, the pitcher is considered "ahead in the count," while the batter is "behind in the count."

• A full-count (three-ball, two-strike) pitch is called the decision pitch, pay ball, payoff pitch, or the one that "tells the tale." If the runners on base move as soon as the pitcher begins to throw the 3-2 pitch, it is considered an "action pitch."

"I managed a team that was so bad we considered a 2-and-0 count on the batter a rally."

- coach/witticist Rich Donnelly

base
n. anchor, anchorage, bag, cushion, hassock, hazard, jute rag, landing, pad, pillow, sack, sandbag, square, station; SPECIFIC empty base, extra base, occupied base, open base, right base, unoccupied base, wrong base; SPANISH almohada, almohadilla

• "Station-to-station" baseball sees an offense advance a series of runners only one base at a time, usually during a sequence of singles.

baseball (the ball)
n. agate, apple, apricot, aspirin, ball, bulb, bun, cantaloupe, casaba, cowhide, egg, globe, globule, grapefruit, hand grenade, hardball, hide, horsehide, leather, lemon, marble, nugget, onion, orange, orb, pearl, pellet, pill, potato, radish, rawhide, rock, sheepskin, sphere, spheroid, stitched potato, tomato; SPANISH bola, pelota

• Sheepskin was used to cover baseballs throughout the

1860s, replaced soon after by the introduction of horsehide. In 1975, the industry switched to cowhide. As George Will writes in *Men at Work,* "The earliest balls were leaden – literally. They were homemade, using little lumps of lead wrapped with twine and covered with animal hide, sometimes chamois or sheepskin. When rubber replaced lead at the core, some balls weighed as little as 3 ounces. But since 1876 the ball had a constant size (9 to 9 ¼ inches in circumference) and weight (5 to 5 ¼ ounces)."

• A "pearl" is a brand-new baseball, perfectly white, and may not be not used in a game until it has been rubbed up with Lena Blackburne Baseball Rubbing Mud to remove its sheen. Blackburne, a Philadelphia Athletics coach, discovered the mud on the shores of the Delaware River near his home in New Jersey in 1938 and introduced it to the American League. Now it is in firm use throughout organized baseball.

• On August 4, 1908, Brooklyn defeated St. Louis 4-0 in a game that only used one baseball. Wrote Cait Murphy in *Crazy '08*: "After the first few innings, it became a sport to keep the thing in play. In the eighth, umpire Bill Klem thinks about replacing the battered orb, but decides what the hell: 'I saw the ball was game and always coming back for more. In order that it might set a record I concluded it would be wise to let the ball play until it wept down and out.' "

"All you have to do is pick up a baseball. It begs to you: Throw me. If you took a year to design an object to hurl, you'd end up with that little spheroid small enough to nestle in your fingers but big enough to have some heft, lighter than a rock but heavier than a hunk of wood. Its even, neat stitching, laced into the leather's slippery white surface, gives your fingers a purchase. A baseball was

made to throw. It's almost irresistible."
– Dave Dravecky with Tom Stafford, *Comeback*

baseball (the sport)
n. America's pastime, ball, ball game, base ball, base-ball, game, game of inches, Grand Ol' Game, hardball, Mudville, national game, national pastime, old ball game, round ball, sport, star-spangled game, summer game, sunshine game, Yankee Doodle game; SPANISH béisbol

• The switch in public usage from "base ball" to "baseball" occurred in the 1930s.

"The one constant through all the years, Ray, has been baseball. America has rolled by like an army of steamrollers. It's been erased like a blackboard, rebuilt, and erased again. But baseball has marked the time."
- James Earl Jones as writer Terence Mann, "Field of Dreams" (1989)

baseball cap
n. cap, hat, headgear, headgear, lid, sky piece (or skypiece), topper; SPANISH gorra

• Known for their distinctive front visors, baseball caps are currently composed of wool or polyester. This was not originally the case – the original Knickerbocker Base Ball Club of New York City wore straw hats when they first started playing the game in 1849.

• The 1860 Brooklyn Excelsiors are credited as the first team to wear a rounded-top cap.

• The protruding front of the baseball cap is the *brim* or *bill.*

It is customarily curved downward over the eyes, though players such as Mike Cameron, George Sherrill, Chad Cordero, and Edinson Volquez prefer to wear their brims perfectly straight.

baseball field
n. ballfield, ballpark, ballyard, baseball park, building, cathedral, coliseum, diamond, digs, establishment, facility, field, garden, ground, grounds, lot, office, orchard, palace, park, pasture, peapatch, playing field, playing grounds, stadium, yard; SPECIFIC baseball-only ballpark, bowl, classic ballpark, classic-style ballpark, dome, double-deck ballpark, multipurpose stadium, oval, playground, retro park, sandlot, single-deck ballpark, state-of-the-art ballpark, superstadium, triple-deck ballpark, upper deck ballpark; INSULTING dump, heap, hole, house of horrors, landfill, mausoleum, sty; SPANISH diamante, estadio, pley

• The placement of the bases in the infield indicates a diamond shape; hence, a baseball "diamond."

• The Spanish *pley* derives from the English word *play*.

• A "Bowl" may sound more like the location for a football game than a baseball game, but the Philadelphia Phillies played their home games in the Baker Bowl from 1887-1938.

• A "multipurpose stadium" is used to host more than just baseball games.

• The Negro Leagues' famous New York Cuban Stars played in the Dyckman Oval in Washington Heights from 1922-1932. In 1930, the Oval became the first ballpark in the state of New York to feature regular night games.

• A "superstadium" referred to the larger ballparks erected in the early decades of the 20th century beginning with Boston's Braves Field in 1915.

• A baseball field where the stadium seats are located close to the diamond is considered *cozy* or "intimate."

"Stadiums are the cathedrals of baseball. Or, in my case, synagogues."

- Billy Crystal

baseball field, home
n. abode, ballwick, crib, domicile, familiar footing, friendly ground, habitat, haunt, haven, home field, home soil, home turf, house, neighborhood, nest, pad, residence, roost, stomping grounds

• *Home* may be placed in front of any of the different terms for a baseball field to denote a team's particular stadium; i.e., home grounds, home orchard, home park.

• The Chicago Cubs play at the "Friendly Confines" of Wrigley Field.

"There are reasons why you sometimes think a player will perform better for you than for the club he's with. Usually it has to do with the architecture of your park."

–Hall of Fame owner Bill Veeck (Cleveland Indians, 1946-1949; St. Louis Browns, 1951-1954; Chicago White Sox, 1959-1980)

baseball field, hitter-friendly
n. bandbox/band box, cigar box, cracker box, flea-box,

hitter's haven, hitter's heaven, hitter's paradise, hitter's park, launching pad

• Atlanta-Fulton County Stadium (1966-1996), the home of the Atlanta Braves before the team moved into Turner Field, was nicknamed the "Launching Pad."

• Minnesota's Hubert H. Humphrey Metrodome (1982-2009) was nicknamed, perhaps unfairly, the "Homer Dome" (or "Homerdome").

• In *Take Me Out to the Ballpark,* Josh Leventhal notes that Lakefront Park, the 19th century home of the Chicago White Stockings, "had the shortest outfield dimensions of any in history, with left field and right field each measuring less than 200 feet from home plate."

baseball field, pitcher-friendly
n. dead zone, Death Valley, graveyard, pitcher's paradise, pitcher's park

• A great many ballparks in the first half of the 20th century had both pitcher-friendly and hitter-friendly elements. The Polo Grounds, home of the New York Giants, presented a distant center field fence ranging from 430 feet to over 480 feet from home plate depending on the season – but the left-field and right-field corners presented dimensions of less than 280 feet. A batter who pulled the ball down the line would find the park to be quite hospitable, but one who slugged a deep fly toward center field would likely head back to the dugout in disappointment.

• No ballpark was more spacious than the first home field in the history of the Boston Red Sox, opening in 1901. "The Huntington Avenue Ball Grounds," writes Leventhal in *Take Me Out to the Ballpark,* "had the deepest center field of any ballpark in Major League history, measuring a staggering 635 feet from home plate."

baseball player
n. ballman, ballplayer, baseballer, baseballist (or ballist), boy/man of summer, charge, diamond artist, diamondeer, field hand, horsehider, jock, SPANISH jugador, pelotero

• The talented and beloved 1940s-1950s Brooklyn Dodgers were nicknamed the "Boys of Summer."

"Nearly everyone's son wants to be a baseball player. Why not? What other profession could he choose where he can slide around in the dirt, never work when it rains and spit wherever he wants?"
– Erma Bombeck, *The Baltimore Sun*; July 15, 1993

baseball player, eccentric
n. cadet, cashew, flake, moonman, nut, screwball, screwjack, space cadet, spaceman, squirrel; SPANISH loco

• Wrote Floyd Conner in *Baseball's Most Wanted*, "Some believe that the term 'flake' derived from a teammate commenting on Jackie Brandt, 'Things seem to flake off his mind and disappear.' Brandt played outfield in the majors from 1956 to 1967. Questioned about his intensity before the 1962 season, Brandt promised, 'This year I'm going to play with harder nonchalance.' He blamed his inconsistent defensive play on the fact that when he ran hard, his eyeballs jumped up and down."

• Left-handed pitchers are often stereotyped as possessing wacky personalities. This is particularly the case if they reside in the bullpen, the natural habitat for the common baseball flake.

• A right-handed pitcher with a peculiar sense of humor and perspective on life, such as Jim "The Mighty Emu" Kern (1974-1986), may be described as a "lefty hiding in a right-hander's body."

• Entering the 1973 season, left-hander Bill "Spaceman" Lee (1969-1982) requested a #337 jersey so that it would spell his last name if he stood on his head.

"You have a left and a right [hemisphere of the brain]. The left side controls the right half of your body, and the right side controls the left half. Therefore, left-handers are the only people in their right mind."

– Bill Lee, SABR collection

baseball player, experienced

n. ancient, elder statesman, graybeard, old guard, old hand, old man, old pro, old salt, old-timer, pro, salty, vet, veteran, warhorse; SPANISH veterano

• retire from baseball

n. bid farewell, bow out, call it a career, call it quits, deliver one's swan song, ease out, give notice, hang it up, hang up one's spikes, head on home, move on with one's life, pack it in, quit, say goodbye, see the writing on the wall, take one's leave, thank for the memories, wind up, wrap it up

• An experienced player is cagey, crafty, "knows the ropes" and the "tricks of the trade," and has "been here before."

"That's the hell of it. You get smart only when you begin getting old."

– pitcher Allie Reynolds (1942-1954)

baseball player, inexperienced
n. babe, buck, budder, busher, bush leaguer, buttercup, call-up, colt, cub, donkey, fresh face, fresh leaguer, gazoonie/gazoony, greenhorn, green pea, hopeful, huckleberry, jay, jelly bean, kid, kindergartner, lamp, meat, neophyte, pineapple, recruit, rook, rookie, schoolboy, yan, yannigan, young buck, youngster, youth; SPANISH novato, principiante

• A "call-up" is a player recently promoted, or "called up," to the Majors from the Minor Leagues.

• "Rookie," a name for someone new and inexperienced, is thought to derive from an insult to new Army recruits. It began to be used regularly in baseball in the 1930s, often spelled "rooky," becoming commonplace by the end of the decade. Before long, "rookie" advanced from baseball jargon into the national vocabulary.

• Hall of Fame manager Casey Stengel called his rookies the "Youth of America."

baseball player, inexperienced; young and touted
n. blue-chipper, can't miss kid, phenom, phenomenon, prospect, sensation, stud; SPANISH prospecto

• Promising young talents are frequently described with religious diction, hyped as the "chosen one," "messiah," or "savior" for their team. Washington Nationals prospect Stephen Strasburg's highly anticipated 2010 debut was nicknamed "Strasmas" by local media and Nats fans. His 2011 return from Tommy John surgery, therefore, was the

"Strasurrection."

• A youth with great baseball instincts is praised as a "natural."

• Gem imagery: A baseball player with great talent but without experience and instincts is said to be "raw," marking him a ways away from the Major Leagues. If he's closer to making his Major League debut, he's "polished."

• A young baseball player is scouted with the long-term prediction of how he'll "project;" that is, what sort of player will he be in five to ten years when his athletic ability is at its peak. A player with great size (upwards of 6'2) is said to have a "projectable frame." A player with "projectable power" is believed to be a true home run hitter someday, even if he isn't one currently. Similarly, scouts search for a player's "ceiling" or "upside." The higher the upside, the higher the player's potential for greatness.

baseball player, inexperienced; hyped but disappointing
n. bomb, bust, fizzle, lemon, pheenom; SPECIFIC bloomer, early bloomer, flash in the pan, june bug, morning glory, one-game wonder, one-hit wonder

• Rube Marquard was smeared as the "The $13,000 Lemon" after the 1908 New York Giants spent the exorbitant sum to sign the 22-year-old, only to see him struggle at the start of his big league career. Marquard recovered to win 20+ games each season from 1911-13 and was inducted into the Hall of Fame in 1971.

• Bloomer, early bloomer, june bug, and morning glory all describe an inexperienced player who impresses early in the season, but struggles as the year wears on. In 2006, the

Detroit Tigers' Chris Shelton slugged nine home runs in his first 13 games but only hit nine more homers the rest of the season and spent the entirety of 2007 back in the Minor Leagues.

• A "flash in the pan" is a player who performs superbly for a short while, but does not produce well in the long run. The New York Yankees' Kevin Maas hit ten home runs in his first 72 at-bats in the Major Leagues in 1990, finishing the season with 21 homers in just 79 games. Eight years later, Yankees' Shane Spencer blasted 10 home runs in the final 27 games of the season. To the disappointment of the Bronx faithful, neither Maas nor Spencer translated that smashing debut to consistent Major League success.

"The worst curse in life is 'unlimited potential.'"
– Ken Brett (1967, 1969-1981)

baseball player, high-energy
n. baseball rat, dirtbag, effort player, hustle player, hustler, scrapper, sparkplug

• A "baseball rat" is a compliment fixed upon a player who loves the game, gives his all, and is perpetually the owner of the dirtiest uniform on the team by the end of each game, earned through sheer force of effort. A baseball rat, as the cliché goes, is the first to arrive at the field each day and the last to leave the field each night.

• The nickname for California State University, Long Beach athletic teams may officially be the 49ers, but the baseball team has incorporated the "Dirtbag" name as its own nickname. The Long Beach State Dirtbags have produced All-Stars Jason Giambi, Jered Weaver, Evan Longoria, and Troy Tulowitzki in addition to a wealth of aspiring Major League talent.

baseball player, able to play many positions
n. handyman, jack of all trades, utility man/utilityman; SPECIFIC fourth outfielder, supersub, super utility

• A "super utility" player is able to competently play many different defensive positions.

• A "supersub" describes an everyday starter who plays multiple defensive positions. The term came into popular use due to Mark McLemore's superb play while starting regularly at one of six different positions for the 2001 Seattle Mariners – left field, center field, right field, third base, second base, and shortstop.

• A "fourth outfielder" is able to play each outfield position, giving any of the three everyday starters a game off at the manager's whim.

• On September 8, 1965, Bert Campaneris of the Kansas City Athletics became the first player in Major League history to play everywhere on the diamond in the same game, spending one inning at each defensive position. The Twins' César Tovar equaled the feat on September 22, 1968, as did two players during the 2000 season, the Rangers' Scott Sheldon on September 6th and the Tigers' Shane Halter on October 1st. As it so happened, Halter doubled in the bottom of the ninth and scored the game-winning run on a Hal Morris RBI single in a wild 12-11 victory over Minnesota.

"I can play anywhere; first, third, left field. Anywhere but Philadelphia."
– slugger Dick Allen (1963-1977), who spent nine of his 15

season with the Phillies

baseball player, non-starter
n. backup, bench polisher, benchwarmer, caddie, dub, humpty-dumpty, irregular, reserve, rider of the lonesome pine, part-timer, part-time player, rinky-dink, role player, scrub, scrubeenie, second stringer; SPECIFIC bullet, pinch-runner, pinch-hitter, platoon player; SPANISH banco, jugador del banco

• A baseball player who receives daily starting assignments is a "regular." Naturally, this renders a bench player "irregular."

• A dangerous pinch-hitter is a manager's "bullet." If a team is trailing at the end of a tense game but has a pair of quality hitters waiting on the bench, the manager has two bullets at his disposal.

• If a team uses a "platoon," two players are alternated in the starting lineup depending upon whether the opposition's starting pitcher is left-handed or right-handed. (A left-handed batter generally hits better against right-handed pitching, and a right-handed batter generally meets great success against left-handed pitching.)

• A baseball player stuck on the bench due to a conflict with the manager is in the "doghouse."

"Bench me or trade me."

– Chico Ruiz (1964-1971)

baseball player, star
n. all-world, beauty, big name, box office draw, cash cow,

dynamo, face of the franchise, fan favorite, franchise player, great, headliner, headline act, hero, icon, idol, jewel, lulu, main draw, marquee attraction, peacherino, standout, stud, superstar, sweetheart; SPANISH jugador estrella

• A "peacherino," referring to a superb player or fantastic play, is traced by Paul Dickson to a reference in the *New York Evening Journal* in 1908.

• The five "tools" of a position player (a non-pitcher) are hit, hit for average, run, field, and throw. A five-tool player ("toolsy" or a "tool shed") excels at each tool, making him a true superstar in the sport. Shortstop-turned-third baseman Alex Rodriguez is an ideal example of such a player.

base hit
n. clipper, knock, poke, safety; SPANISH batazo, imparable

• If a batter reaches only first base on his base hit, he receives a single. Two bases is a double, three bases is a triple, and all four bases is a home run. See *single*, *double*, *triple*, or *home run* for more specific terms for each.

• An extra-base hit refers to any hit other than a single.

• A batter "hits for the cycle" when he collects a single, double, triple, and home run in the same game.

• A double or a triple that does not require the batter to slide is a "stand-up" double/triple (as opposed to a "sliding" or "hustle" double/triple).

• A "clipper" may be a base hit, but according to Richard Ben Cramer, Yankee legend Joe DiMaggio (1936-1942,

1946-1951) was nicknamed "The Yankee Clipper" by PA announcer Arch McDonald for his exemplary gliding range in the outfield, connecting it to the Pan Am "Clipper."

• Perennial Mariners All-Star outfielder Ichiro Suzuki set the Major League record for most base hits in a season with 262 knocks in 2004, breaking Hall of Famer George Sisler's (1915-1930) 1920 mark of 257.

• On July 10, 1932, Cleveland Indians shortstop Johnny Burnett (1927-1935) collected nine hits in 11 at-bats to set the Major League record for most base hits in one ballgame. The achievement came in a losing cause as Burnett's Indians fell to the Philadelphia Athletics 18-17 in 18 innings. The game victory featured 58 total base hits, 33 by Cleveland. The record for most hits in a nine-inning game is seven, held by Wilbert Robinson (June 10, 1892) and Rennie Stennett (September 16, 1975).

"To a pitcher a base hit is the perfect example of negative feedback."

– outfielder Steve Hovley (1969-1973), as quoted by Jim Bouton in *Ball Four*

basepath

n. avenue, bag path, lane, path, runway, towpath; SPANISH camino de la base, linea de la base

"90 feet between the bases is the nearest thing to perfection that man has yet achieved."

– New York sportswriter Walter "Red" Smith

baserunner

n. man aboard, man on, runner, tenant; SPANISH corredor

• A baserunner at second or third base is in "scoring position," since they should be able to score on a single.

• A player who reaches base is "aboard." Should a couple of players reach, particularly if they are in scoring position, they are "ducks on the pond."

• A baserunner rounds or circles the bases as he advances around the diamond, "making the turn" at each bag.

• A "kangaroo" runs the bases with a leaping gait; "kangaroo hops" refer to the act of taking a lead from a base.

• A baserunner who gets picked off is said to have fallen asleep, strayed, or been caught napping.

• A "missile" or "torpedo" is a baserunner who goes hard into a base, barreling into or roll-blocking a fielder in order to break up a play.

• In 1973, the designated hitter was instituted in the American League. A year later, flamboyant Oakland Athletics owner Charlie O. Finley introduced the "designated runner." Michigan State product Herb Washington, then 22 years old, was a celebrated sprinter, and Finley was convinced the speed would translate on the baseball diamond. Washington took part in 92 games in 1974 and 13 more games in 1975, all of them as a pinch-runner. He stole only 31 bases in 48 attempts, was famously picked off first base by Dodgers pitcher Mike Marshall in the 1974 World Series, and never once came to the plate in the Major Leagues. Undeterred by Washington's lack of success, the A's next signed Don Hopkins. The 23-year-old Hopkins stole 21 bases and scored 25 runs in 82 games in 1975 and took part in three more games in 1976 before calling it a career.

"Speed is a great asset; but it's greater when combined with quickness – and there's a big difference."
– Hall of Fame outfielder Ty Cobb (1905-1928)

baserunner, fast
n. blue streak, blur, burner, cheetah, deer, flash, flyer, gazelle, greased lightning, jackrabbit, jet, rabbit, speed demon, speed merchant, speedster, whirlwind, zebra; SPANISH vuela

• Many of the above terms may similarly be applied to a similarly speedy fielder.

• A player with great speed is said to have "great wheels" or "jets," "picking them up and putting them down" and/or shifting into "high gear" as he makes his way around the bases.

• A fast baseball player may be categorized as accelerated, daring, electric, flashing, fleet, fleet-footed, flying, hasty, hypersonic, in a hurry, lightning fast (or quick), lively, mercurial, nimble, quick, rapid, speedy, sudden, supersonic, swift, velocious, winged, or world-class.

• In more folksy terms, a player blessed with great speed may be as quick as a flash, quick as a wink, or quicker than a hiccup. In more technical terms, he may have great reflexes, a quick first step, or have fast-twitch (or fast twitch) athleticism/muscles/fibers.

• A fast runner who gets off to a fast start (also known as a "jump") on his way to the next base looks like he's been "shot out of a cannon."

• A "bug on a rug" is a fast runner on artificial turf.

• In Spanish, *volar* is "to fly." A *vuela* is a "flyer."

• If a number of fast players are grouped together on the same team, it is said that they have great "team speed." A team like the 1980s St. Louis Cardinals, who featured stolen base threats Vince Coleman, Willie McGee, and Ozzie Smith, was said to turn a baseball game into a track meet.

• In the world of baseball lore, no one was as swift as switch-hitting James "Cool Papa" Bell (1922-1950), Negro League legend and Hall of Fame outfielder, inspiring tales of his exploits wherever he played. As one yarn went, "Cool Papa Bell was so fast, he could switch off the light and be under the covers in his bed before the room got dark."

"[Bell] was so fast that opposing players had trouble believing their eyes when they saw him run. Jimmie Crutchfield recalls that when 'Bell hit back to the pitcher, everybody would yell, "Hurry!" ' And Judy Johnson said that when Bell was at bat with no one on base, the infielders moved in as if a man were on third with one out."
– Robert Peterson, *Only the Ball was White*

baserunner, slow
n. base-clogger, elephant, piano mover, plodder, rhinoceros, sloth, slug, snail, truck horse, turtle; SPANISH camion

• The antithesis of "Cool Papa" Bell was Hall of Fame

catcher Ernie Lombardi (1931-1947). Lombardi was legendary for his lethal bat, his enormous nose (which protruded through his catcher's mask), his loud snoring, and his utter lack of anything resembling foot speed. By 1939, a year after he earned the National League's Most Valuable Player Award, infielders throughout the league began to defend him successfully from the outfield grass.

"The pressure is off now."

– Detroit slugger Cecil Fielder after stealing his first career base on April 2, 1996. The stolen base came in big Cecil's 1,096th career game, a Major League record.

bases loaded

n. bases bulging, bases choked, bases clogged, bases crammed, bases crowded, bases drunk, bases full, bases jammed, bases juiced, bases packed, bases stocked, bases tenanted, bases waterlogged, full house, man at every base, sacks full, sold out; SPANISH bases llena

• "Bags" may replace "bases" in any of the above phrases.

• If the bases are loaded, the offensive team "has the pitcher surrounded."

• If a pitcher falls behind in the count to a batter with the bases loaded, it's likely you'll hear the broadcaster say, "There's no place to put him." After all, a walk forces in a run.

• A base hit with the bases loaded leading to all three runners scoring is said to "clear," "clean," or "unload" the bases.

• A home run with the bases loaded is a "grand slam." (See

grand slam.)

bat

n. ax (or axe), ball club, ball-hitter, baton, betsy, biff stick, bludgeon, boat oar, chopstick, club, cudgel, crutch, dues collector, fagot, flail, hickory, leather-beater, log, lumber, mace, moneymaker, oak, oar, paddle, pencil, pestle, pole, rod, shillelagh, shillelah, stick, swat stick, timber, tree, tree trunk, twig, wagon spoke, wand, war club, weapon, whooping stick, willow, wood; SPECIFIC aluminum bat, ash, banana stalk, banana stick, Big Bertha, Black Betsy, bottle bat, broken bat, cold bat, crack, cracked bat, cupped bat, dynamite bat, fat bat, fungo, fungo bat, fungo stick, gamer, graphite bat, helicopter, hot bat, iron bat, lead bat, live bat, Louisville slugger, magic wand, maple, morning journal, pea shooter, piece of iron, pine tar bat, rubber bat, sawed-off bat, seeing-eye bat, slow bat, slugger, swatstick, tipped bat, toothpick, wagon tongue; SPANISH bate

• The thick top of the bat is known as the barrel, head, or fat part. A ball that hits just right on the barrel is said to hit the "sweet spot."

• The label (or trademark) is the branded or printed manufacturer's name. Batters are taught to never hit the ball on the label, printed on the weakest part of the wood.

• The bottom end of a bat is the handle. At the bottom of the handle is the knob. A batter "choking up" on a bat brings his hands higher up the handle in order to shorten his swing and swing faster.

• A batter's hands are customarily placed with the hand farthest away from the pitcher placed higher on the handle (for example, a right-handed hitter places his right hand higher than his left hand). If a batter does the opposite, putting the closer hand on top, it is considered a "cross-handed grip." Hall of Fame outfielder Hank Aaron (1954-1976) was notable for learning to hit with a cross-handed grip.

• Two different metaphors are often used in describing a player bringing his/her bat to the plate:

1. The bat as a heavy burden: carry, haul, heft, hoist, lug, shoulder, tote.
2. The bat as a sword: brandish, flaunt, flourish, wave menacingly (or threateningly), wield.

• A "two-toned" bat has a different color for its handle and its barrel, usually an unstained handle with a darker-stained barrel.

• A black bat is said to have a "Foster Finish," named after outfielder George Foster (1969-1986). A brown bat is said to have a "Hornsby Finish" for Hall of Fame second baseman Rogers Hornsby (1915-1937). A two-toned bat with a black barrel and light handle is said to have a "Gwynn Finish" for Hall of Fame outfielder Tony Gwynn (1982-2001).

• In addition to being one of the best defensive players of his time, Cincinnati Reds third baseman Henry "Heinie" Groh (1912-1927) used a specially made "bottle bat" with a thin handle and a long evenly-thick barrel, more closely resembling a modern softball bat or fungo stick. The unique barrel enabled Groh to become a top-notch leadoff man for the Cincinnati's 1919 World Series Champions (though it helped somewhat that the Reds' American League opponents that year were the crooked Chicago Black Sox, who had seven players banned from baseball for throwing the Series and one more, Buck Weaver, banned for knowing of the conspiracy).

• When a bat breaks, it may burst, chip, crack, fracture, part, rupture, shatter, snap, splinter, or split. An illegal corked bat tends to explode or "come unglued."

• If a bat flies out of the batter's hands, "helicoptering" end over end through the air, it is called a "wild duck."

• A "magic wand" is a bat that grants a hitter a sizable amount of base hits.

bat, illegal
n. SPECIFIC cheater, corked bat, doctored bat, hollow bat, plugged bat, poisoned bat

• Television's "Mythbusters" dedicated an episode to testing the idea that a corked bat (that is, a bat whose barrel has been hollowed out and filled with cork) hits a baseball better than an uncorked bat. Defying its reputation, the illegal bat did not demonstrate any advantage over its legal cousin.

"I'm going to get myself a corked bat and blast one out of here. What's the suspension for Old-Timers games, 10 years?"

– outfielder Vada Pinson (1958-1975), before an Old-Timers' Day game

batter
n. apple-knocker, baton swinger, batsman, batsmith, biffer, bludgeon wielder, clubber, goal tender, hitsman, hitsmith, hitter, lumberjack, sticker, stickman, sticksmith, striker, stroker, swatsman, swatsmith, swatster, swatter, swinger,

wood carrier; SPANISH bateador, pelotero

• A batter may stand at home plate with an even stance (feet equally close to the plate), and open stance (front foot farther away than the back foot), or a closed stance (back foot farther from the plate than the front foot).

• A stance is considered "quiet" if the batter remains as still as possible before the pitch.

• If the batter waves the bat back and forth while awaiting the pitch, he's using a "trigger mechanism" to help him with his timing.

• If the batter stands as close to the plate as he can, the batter is said to be "crowding" or "standing on top of" the plate.

• A batter stepping into the batter's box may be said to be "climbing" in.

• If the batter tries to get a good foothold with his spikes, it is considered "digging" in.

• A batter who is patient at the plate and takes a lot of pitches before swinging is a "looker," "surveyor," or "waiter."

• If the batter has a good eye for the strike zone, he possesses a "hawk eye" or "camera eye."

• A "mistake hitter" is a batter who feasts on poorly thrown pitches.

• A "bad-ball hitter" is a batter who is able to effectively hit pitches outside the strike zone.

• A “free swinger” or “hacker” is a batter who swings often, even at poor pitches.

• A “Statue of Liberty,” “soldier,” or “window-shopper” is a batter who strikes out looking.

• A human rain delay” is a batter who takes an inordinate amount of time delaying at home plate in between pitches. Mike Hargrove (1974-1985) was the original “Human Rain Delay,” going through a notable routine of tugs, hitches, and uniform adjustments between every pitch. The pitching version of Hargrove was right-hander Steve Trachsel (1993-2008), who saw no need to rush himself between pitches, particularly with runners on base, and tended to draw out every game he worked.

batter, powerful
n. basher, belter, big bat, bomber, bopper, clouter, fencebuster, heavy hitter, home run hitter, long-ball hitter, lumberjack, masher, monster, muscle man, power hitter, powerhouse, power threat, slugger, slugsmith, socker, thumper; SPANISH jonronero

• A powerful lineup is a “wrecking crew” or a “murderer’s row.” The original “Murderer’s Row” were the 1927 New York Yankees, who swept their way to a World Championship behind a lineup featuring Babe Ruth, Lou Gehrig, Tony Lazzeri, and Earle Combs.

• A batter who hits a great deal of home runs is a “prodigious” home run hitter.

• A batter who hits a great deal of home runs but also strikes out regularly is an “all-or-nothing” hitter.

• Weight-training has been unpopular throughout baseball history, but one of the earliest proponents of the exercise was Hall of Fame Pittsburgh Pirates shortstop Honus Wagner (1897-1917). It all worked out well for the talented "Flying Dutchman," who led the league in batting average eight times, doubles seven times, slugging percentage six times, and both RBIs and stolen bases five times.

• When it came to pure power, few sluggers cut an imposing figure like 6'7, 255-pound Frank "Hondo" Howard (1958-1973). Playing in a pitcher's era and in pitcher's parks, Howard flexed his muscles to the tune of 382 home runs in his career. As Joe Posnanski wittily penned, "Frank Howard used to scare home runs out of the park."

"The pitcher has got only a ball. I've got a bat. So the percentage in weapons is in my favor and I let the fellow with the ball do the fretting."

– Hall of Famer Hank Aaron (1954-1976), *Milwaukee Journal;* July 31, 1956

batter, far from powerful

n. banjo hitter, contact hitter, Judy, parachute hitter, place hitter, Punch-and-Judy, sharpshooter, singles hitter, slap hitter, ukulele hitter; SPANISH jitero

• A singles hitter generally has a short or "compact" swing.

• An effective singles hitter is a "pest" or a "piranha."

• Philadelphia's Roy Thomas (1899-1911) was a terrific leadoff hitter and stolen-base artist who rarely, if ever, collected anything more than a single. Thomas recorded

168 base hits in 1900: four doubles, three triples, no homers, and a boatload of singles. His hits in 1902 numbered 143, of which only four were doubles and seven were triples. Three years later, he doubled 11 times, tripled six times, and singled 161 times. Thomas ended his solid 13-year career with a fine .290 batting average and sterling .413 on-base percentage thanks to 1,377 singles but only 160 extra-base hits.

batter, talented
n. expert, machine, natural, professional hitter, pure hitter, violinist, wood man (or woodman); SPANISH bateador profesional, buen bateador

• It's said that a "professional hitter" has so much talent at the plate, he could roll out of bed and collect a base hit.

• Hall of Fame second baseman Charlie Gehringer (1924-1942) was nicknamed "The Mechanical Man" for both his silent manner and, as Detroit Tigers teammate Doc Cramer put it, "You wind him up [at the start of the season] and forget him." The consistent and dependable Gehringer reached the 200-hit plateau in seven different seasons, batting .320 in his career.

"Hitting is an art, but not an exact science."
– Hall of Famer Rod Carew (1967-1985)

batter, untalented
n. All-American out, automatic out, buttercup, cake, cherry, cherry pie, cupcake, dub, easy out, fish, ham hitter, hopeless cause, humpty-dumpty, light bat, locust hitter, lulu, out man, monkey, no batter, sandblower, Stetson hitter, tickle hitter, Yankee Doodle hitter; SPANISH bateador

malo

• A poor batter (or a poor hitting team) is declared "punchless" and "couldn't hit his way out of a paper bag."

• A Stetson hitter's hat size matches his batting average.

• A batter especially does not want to hit his weight or his bowling average, two other common denigrations... that is, unless he's grossly overweight or tremendously skilled at the bowling alley.

• A batter "on the interstate" is hitting between .100 and .199, since .195 looks like I-95 (Interstate 95), etc. If a batter's batting average is below .100, well, he's "off the map."

• A baseball player with a batting average near .200 is said to be flirting with the "Mendoza Line," named for legendarily weak-hitting shortstop Mario Mendoza (1974-1982). Still, Mendoza did manage to bat a cool .215 in his career, including campaigns of .245 in 1980, .231 in 1981, and .221 in his rookie year of 1974.

"It's no fun throwing fastballs to guys who can't hit them. The real challenge is getting them out on stuff they can hit."

– "Sudden" Sam McDowell (1961-1975)

batting cage
n. cage

• The large batting cage (sometimes cages), where hitters work on their swings before, after, and during games, is located beneath the stands in all Major League stadiums and an assortment of Minor League ballparks. In others, it can be found beyond the outfield wall or outside the ballpark entirely.

• A pitching machine, often found in the batting cage, is nicknamed “Iron Mike.”

batting practice
n. BP, cuts, swings

• A “five o’clock hitter” is a batter who only looks good during batting practice. This term may be adjusted to better reflect the time that a team takes batting practice, whether closer to four o’clock or six o’clock.

• It is considered highly embarrassing to break one’s bat in batting practice – but it’s even more embarrassing to borrow and then break a teammate’s bat.

• Each set of batting practice swings for a player is known as a “round.” There are different types of rounds: A situational “2-2-2 round,” for instance, sees a batter take two swings to move a hypothetical runner from first to second base, two swings to move the runner from second to third base, and two swings to drive them in. A “base hit round” allows a batter to remain at the plate as long as he continues to collect base hits (their validity judged by his coaches and teammates). A “home run round” sees a player attempt to hit as many home runs as he can in a set number of swings.

bleachers
n. cheap seats, gallery, grandstand, nosebleeds, peanut gallery, Ruthville, scorchers, seats, souvenir seats, stands, Uecker seat, upper deck; SPANISH gradas

• "Nosebleeds" are bleachers located so far away from the field and so high in the air that they give fans nosebleeds due to the altitude.

• 'Scorchers' are bleachers situated in the sun, likely causing more sunburns than tans.

• A "Uecker seat" is a bleacher seat that is as far as possible from home plate, named for catcher, humorist, actor, and Milwaukee Brewers broadcaster Bob Uecker after a memorable appearance in a Miller Lite commercial, where Uecker thought he was being escorted to the ballpark's front row and instead planted in the back row of the bleachers. There really are Uecker Seats in the bleachers at Milwaukee's Miller Park; naturally, they're obstructed view, priced at $1 apiece.

• If the bleachers beyond the outfield wall are closer than usual, allowing easy home runs, they're considered a "short porch." This does not include Fenway Park's famous Green Monster in left field, which stands only 304-310 feet from home plate at an intimidating 37 feet, two inches tall.

blooper pitch
n. balloon, balloon pitch, bloop curve, blooper, Bugs Bunny curve, dewdrop, Eephus, gondola, gravity curve, parachute, soap bubble

• The Eephus was a trick pitch created by Truett "Rip" Sewell (1932, 1938-1949), the cousin of Hall of Famer Joe Sewell, and named by teammate Maurice Van Robays. It would rise some 25 feet above the ground before slowly arcing its way toward the plate. Sewell first used the Eephus in an exhibition game with the Pirates against the

Tigers in 1942.

• Famously, Ted Williams saw three straight Eephuses from Sewell in the 1946 All-Star Game, launching the third into the Fenway Park bleachers for a home run. Later, photographs revealed that Williams had run up toward the pitch, stepping out of the batter's box, and should have been ruled out.

• Modern pitchers of the Eephus include Steve Hamilton and his "folly floater," Dave LaRoche and his "La Lob," Bill Lee and his "Space Ball," Pascual Perez and his "Pascual Pitch," and Casey Fossum and his "Fossum Flip."

• Dodgers broadcaster Vin Scully coined the term "soap bubble" with regard to Vicente Padilla's Eephus variation.

broadcaster
n. announcer, commentator, painter of the picture, storyteller, talker, voice; SPANISH narrador

• The play-by-play broadcaster is the host of the broadcast and is in charge of detailing the direct action of the contest (the "call of the game").

• The color commentator, usually a former player or coach, is expected to provide anecdotes, analysis, and insight.

• A radio or television broadcaster who possesses an excellent voice has "great pipes." On the other hand, a broadcaster without the best pipes has a "voice for newspaper," an insult delivered hand in hand with having "a face for radio."

• A biased broadcaster is a "house man" or a "homer." (A

homer may also refer insultingly to an umpire or official scorer whose calls appear to favor the home team.)

• The very first baseball radio broadcaster was Harold Arlin, a *Pittsburgh Post-Gazette* scribe, who was granted a one-night-only broadcast on KDKA to call the Pirates/Phillies game at Forbes Field in Pittsburgh on August 5, 1921. The Pirates won the game, 8-5, as the 25-year-old Arlin called the action into a microphone that had been converted from a telephone. As it happened, Harold Arlin also broadcast the very first college football game on the radio, a gridiron battle between West Virginia University and the University of Pittsburgh that ensuing autumn.

"With radio... you come into the booth, and there's an empty canvas. And you get all your paint and brushes, and you mix your paints. And then you have a broad swath here and fine line there. And at the end of three hours, you say, 'Well, that's the best I can do today.' On television, you walk in and the picture's already there. So what you're doing is shading, subtle things."

– broadcasting icon Vin Scully, *Boston Globe;* November 25, 2003

bullpen (location)
n. bully, pen, substation, warming pan

• The home and visiting bullpens may be located past each team's dugout down the foul line or beyond the outfield walls. A bullpen down the line carries the benefit of closer proximity to the dugout, but also presents the danger of injury to a hustling fielder chasing a foul ball over the bullpen pitcher's mounds.

• As Dan Schlossberg writes in *Baseball Gold*, "The word *bullpen* became part of the baseball lexicon in the 19th century. Theories for its adoption include: 1) Relief pitchers warmed up near an outfield sign advertising Bull Durham tobacco; 2) Enclosures used by pioneers to protect themselves were called bullpens; 3) In bullfighting, bulls are kept in pens and let out one at a time; 4) Railroad worker shanties, where they rested during breaks, were called bullpens." (Numbers added by author, replacing Schlossberg's bullet points.)

• Relief pitchers nowadays jog or walk in from the bullpen when called upon, same as they did in professional baseball's first 75 years. Then things changed. "It was sometime in the 1950s," explains Peter Handrinos in *The Funniest Baseball Book Ever,* "when some sharp-minded promoters started using automobiles to bring relievers from the outfield bullpen areas to the mound. The White Sox probably started it off with their use of station wagons.... As the years followed, different teams put different spins on bullpen cars. The Brewers acknowledged their blue-collar fans by bringing relievers in on Harley-Davidson motorcycles, Philadelphia brought their 'firemen' into ball games on mini-firetrucks, and the 1970s-era Yankees decided to finally introduce their own ride, a flashy pinstriped Datsun. To this day, in Japan, that leading car exporter, they still have relievers come in on cars, new models advertising both their team ties and their green fuel efficiency."

"Bullpen conversations cover the gambit of male bull sessions. Sex, religion, politics, sex. Full circle. Occasionally, the game – or business – of baseball intrudes."

– Jim Brosnan (1954, 1956-1963), *The Long Season*

bullpen (the pitchers)
n. arms in reserve, pen, relief arms, relief corps, relief crew, relievers

• See *relief pitcher.*

"I've come to the conclusion that the two most important things in life are good friends and a good bullpen."
– Hall of Famer Bob Lemon (1946-1958)

bunt
n. baby act, baby hit; SPECIFIC bunt single, drag bunt, push bunt, sacrifice, slug bunt, safety squeeze, squeeze, suicide squeeze, surprise bunt; SPANISH toque de bola
v. deaden, drag, drop down, dump, get down, lay one down, place, plop, push, sacrifice

"I've got nothing against the bunt – in its place. But most of the time, that place is in the bottom of a long-forgotten closet."
– Hall of Fame manager Earl Weaver (1968-1982, 1985-1986)

• show bunt
v. pivot, slide a hand up the handle, square, square around

• In a bunt, the batter moves his top hand up the bat handle in order to purposefully hit the ball lightly on the ground, intending either for a base hit or to advance a baserunner (called a "sacrifice," since the batter is giving himself up for the benefit of his teammate).

• A "push bunt" is a bunt directed to the opposite side of the field from the batter, as when a right-hander bunts toward the right side of the infield. A "drag bunt" is the exact opposite, executed by a left-handed hitter bunting the ball directly down the first-base line.

• A batter still slides his hand up the handle of the bat for a "slug bunt" but swings away nonetheless, slapping the ball past a drawn-in (and very surprised) infielder.

• A "squeeze" occurs with a baserunner at third base. A "suicide squeeze" sees the runner racing madly for home as soon as the pitcher releases the pitch, putting the pressure on the batter to execute the bunt or else "hang his teammate out to dry," allowing an easy out for the defense. A "safety squeeze" sees the runner cautiously wait to see the result of the batter's bunt attempt before venturing toward the plate.

• A "swinging bunt" is not a purposeful bunt at all. It occurs when a batter's full swing manages barely any contact, with the ball dribbling in front of home plate or down a line just like a bunt.

"There is no reason why a Major League batter should not be able to bunt. But too many of them fail. This is largely because they dislike to bunt and won't take the trouble to learn....It's an important play quite apart from its value in the sacrifice. It's the best possible weapon to break up speed pitching which you can't hit. It's always an ace in your sleeve at a critical time."

– Hall of Famer George Sisler (1915-1930)

C

Roger Patrick Bresnahan, catcher for the New York Giants. *(Courtesy Library of Congress, LC-USZ62-97878.)*

catch

n. collection, grab, haul, pick, reception, snag, snatch, spear, squeeze, stab, stick; SPECIFIC a la carte, backhand, backhand stab, barehand, basket catch, breadbasket catch, diving catch, fly catch, hip-pocket catch, ice cream cone, one-hand catch, over-the-shoulder catch, running catch, scoop, shoestring catch, sliding catch, sno-cone/snow cone, two-hand catch, vest-pocket catch; SPANISH atrapada (trap), jugada

v. accept, acquire, backhand, backhand stab, bag, barehand, bring in, capture, chase down, clasp, clutch, collar, collect, corral, dig, drink, eat up, fetch, field, flag down, freeze, gain, gather, glove, gobble, grab, grasp, handle, haul in, hoover, hug, intercept, latch hold of, nab, obtain, pick, pick up, pluck, pounce on, procure, put away, rake in, receive, reel in, rob, scoop, secure, seize, snag, snatch, snow cone, spear, squeeze, stab, steal, stick with backhand, swallow, take, track down, trap, vacuum

• "A la carte" refers to a catch made with one hand.

• A "basket catch" is caught at a fielder's waist/belly as if the fielder used a basket instead of a glove. Hall of Famer Willie Mays (1951-1973) was noted for his basket catches.

• A "shoestring catch" is a running catch made by reaching down to snag the ball from right near a fielder's shoe.

• A "hip-pocket catch" or "vest-pocket catch" is made so easily, the fielder could have caught the ball in his pocket.

• An "ice cream cone" or a "sno-cone" is a catch where the ball peeks out the top of the glove, looking very much like an ice-cream cone or a sno-cone.

• When a fielder "traps" the ball, he catches between his glove and the field's surface, thereby negating a "clean" (legitimate) catch.

• In describing a catch, the ball may be said to "fall (or "drop") out of the sky" into a fielder's glove. If it is raining, a fielder "catches a few raindrops" along with the baseball.

• If a fielder reaches out blindly/instinctively and catches a hard line drive, it's said that "the ball caught him," and is described humorously by the classic exclamation, "Look what I found!"

• In baseball history, there's only one play described as "The Catch." In Game 1 of the 1954 World Series, Cleveland Indians first baseman Vic Wertz came to the plate with the game tied at 2-2 in the top of the eighth inning. Wertz crushed a fly ball over 400 feet to center field, only to see the New York Giants' Willie Mays track the ball down on a dead sprint with an over-the-shoulder catch. The Giants went on to win the game in ten innings, 5-2, on a Dusty Rhodes pinch-hit three-run homer, igniting a four-game sweep of the favored Indians. Wertz, by the way, finished Game 1 with four hits in five at-bats – "The Catch" was the only time the Giants retired him. He batted a stellar .500 in the Series, with eight hits in 16 at-bats.

catch, prepare to
v. anticipate, await, camp under, draw a bead on, pitch a tent, set up shop, wait for

• When a fielder prepares to catch a pop fly or fly ball, he loudly "calls for it" or "calls off" his teammates so as to prevent a collision.

• An "angel" is a cloud that helps a fielder judge how high a pop fly or fly ball is. A "high sky" (one without clouds) hampers a fielder's judgment on the ball's altitude.

• The wind has been known to "play tricks" with pop flies.

• A fielder struggling underneath a fly ball or pop fly is said to "stagger under" or "dance with" the ball.

catch, spectacular
n. beauty, circus catch, corker, dandy, Dunlap, firecracker,

highlight, highway robbery, Jawn Titus, miracle, peacherino, web gem, wonder; SPANISH buena jugada

• At the turn of the 20th century, a "corker" referred to anything spectacular, whether a brilliant catch, a talented player, or an outstanding team.

• "Dunlap" and "Jawn Titus" are both archaic terms describing magnificent catches. A "Dunlap" is named for the defensive wizardry of second baseman Fred Dunlap (1880-1891). The origin of a "Jawn Titus" is unknown, though it may well derive from the play of outfielder John Titus (1903-1912).

• A baseball player who makes a fine defensive play is said to have "flashed leather."

• ESPN's Baseball Tonight crowns the top defensive plays each night as "web gems."

catcher
n. backstop, backstopper, battery mate (or batterymate), behind, blocker, catch, grabber, hind snatcher, mask man, masked man, masker, paddist, pegger, plate blocker, receiver, signal caller, stopper, wind paddist; SPANISH receptor

• The catcher catches the game while in a "crouch" or in the "chair position."

• In order to "buy" a called strike, the catcher may "frame" the pitch, catching it in such a way that the ball appears to be in the strike zone and giving the umpire a good look at it. A poor "frame-job" sees the catcher reach across his body or conspicuously catch a pitch and pull it back toward the zone.

• The catcher (as well as the home-plate umpire) may be said to be in a "rocking chair" if the pitcher is particularly masterful that day.

• The catcher is said to wear "the tools of ignorance," though the equipment is clearly not contagious. A high percentage of notable past and current Major League managers are former catchers, including Hall of Famers Connie Mack, Al Lopez, and Wilbert Robinson and modern-era skippers such as Jim Leyland, Joe Torre, Mike Scioscia, Joe Maddon, and Joe Girardi.

• On a close play at the plate, a catcher may block, guard, protect, or shield the plate from the incoming baserunner. It's all legal as long as the catcher has the ball in his possession.

"His legs are buckled into clumsy shin guards; his face is hidden by the metal grille of a heavy mask....His chest is covered with a corrugated protective pad, and his big mitt is thrust out as if to fend off destruction...his field of vision gives him his own special view of the vast ballpark. In a sense, the game belongs to him. He is the catcher."
– *Time* magazine; August 8, 1955

• **catch stealing**
v. arrest, collar, cut down, erase, gun down, hang out to dry, nab, nail, nip, peg, poach

• **prevent a poor pitch from going astray**
v. backhand, block, dig out, dive upon, halt, kick save, jackknife, lunge, save, slide, smother, sprawl, stop

• **transmit signs (or signals) to the pitcher**

v. deliver, flash, lay down, place down, relay, send, signal

• If the pitcher does not like the sign, he "shakes it off."

• When a pitcher brushes his glove against his chest, he wants the catcher to go back through the signals.

change-up/changeup
n. change, change of pace, let-up pitch, off-speed, parachute, slow ball, switch-pitch, yo-yo; SPECIFIC circle change, foshball, fosh change, four-seam change, split-finger/split-fingered change, slip pitch, straight change, two-seam change, vulcan change; SPANISH cambio

• pitch a change-up
v. fade, hover, pull the string, sink, take a little something off, yo-yo

• A change-up is thrown out of the same arm angle and delivery as a fastball, with the grip of the baseball serving as the most significant difference between the two pitches, slowing the change-up's velocity to ideally eight miles-per-hour less than the fastball on its way plateward. (The ideal change-up for a 92-mph fastball, therefore, would arrive home at 84 mph). A well-thrown change-up throws a hitter off-balance, getting his weight out on his front foot and provoking a far-too-early swing.

• A change-up without any movement is considered a "straight change," fooling the batter only through its difference in velocity.

• A "circle change" is held with the thumb and index finger forming a circle to the left side of the ball and able to be spun off of his middle, ring, or pinkie finger, thereby controlling the pitch's movement.

• A "split-finger change" is thrown with the index and middle fingers spread out to each side of the baseball, stretching the ligaments, and provides natural sinking action. It's a relative of the split-finger fastball. The pitch was called a "foshball" or "fosh change" in the 1980s and 1990s, credited first to Mike Boddicker in his rookie year with the Baltimore Orioles in 1983.

• A two-seam change" tends to sink and/or move to one side ("run") on its way to the plate, similar to the path taken by a "two-seam fastball."

• A "vulcan change" is thrown with the middle finger and ring finger spread to the sides of the ball, causing the ball to sink in addition to slowing down its velocity. The pitch received its name thanks to the grip's similarity to Spock's "Live long and prosper" hand sign from *Star Trek*.

• Hall of Famer Tim Keefe (1880-1893) won 342 games in his career, his success coming in no small part to the new pitch he added to his arsenal in 1883, leading to 359 strikeouts that season. Keefe is considered to be the pioneer of the modern change-up.

closer
n. bullpen ace, cork, finisher, fireman, hoser, ice man, relief ace, sandman, stopper, terminator; SPANISH cerrador

• receive the save, as a pitcher
v. capture, clinch, lock down, nail down, notch, pick up, pin down, seal, secure; SPANISH cerrar, salvar

• A closer is brought into a game with a slim lead in order

to record the final outs, also known as "nailing it down," "shutting the door," or 'turning off the lights."

• Having a top pitcher serve as a weapon out of the bullpen was a ludicrous notion for much of baseball history, only taking root throughout the Major Leagues in the 1960s and 1970s. Forty years earlier, Fred "Firpo" Marberry (1923-1936) served as the pioneer for the archetype, starring for Washington out of the bullpen while pitching sparingly as a starter. (MLB didn't adopt the save as an official stat until 1969, so baseball historians have gone back to the record books to compile retroactive historical save totals.) At a time when the National League leader in saves was recording no more than six in a season, Marberry notched 15 saves in both 1924 and 1925 before posting 22 saves in 1926.

• It took 23 years for another Major League reliever to reach at least 20 saves in a season after Firpo Marberry. Thanks to his "hopping" fastball, New York Yankees fireballer "Fireman" Joe Page (1944-1950, 1954) earned three All-Star nods and respect not usually accorded to a relief pitcher. In 1949, he recorded 27 saves, earning himself a third-place finish for the AL Most Valuable Player Award. He was demoted to the minors a season later, however, and made only a brief unsuccessful return in 1954 with the woeful Pittsburgh Pirates before calling it a career.

• Bespectacled Tom Henke (1982-1995) earned the nickname "The Terminator" in Toronto, recording five saves in the 1992 postseason for the Blue Jays' first World Series Championship. In his final season, the 37-year-old Henke notched 36 saves with a 1.82 ERA for the St. Louis Cardinals.

clubhouse

n. quarters; SPECIFIC coaches' office, dressing room, locker area, manager's office, showers, trainer's room, workout room

• The clubhouse is where players eat, shower, dress, relax, play cards, watch television, receive treatment, and generally prepare for the game. (It is never called the *locker room*, a term which belongs to nearly every other sport.)

• There is no set location for the clubhouse. Some stadiums have their clubhouses built in the current Major League fashion, situated at field level under the stadium seating and connected via narrow hallway to the dugouts. The clubhouses at Riverwalk Stadium in Montgomery, Alabama, are located on top of one another, with the visitors clubhouse at field level and the home clubhouse at concourse level. Other parks have their clubhouses located in permanent buildings, temporary structures, or trailers, either beyond the center field wall or outside the stadium entirely. Then there's the visitors clubhouse at Champion Window Field, home of the independent Florence (Kentucky) Freedom, which is situated up a hill and down the road, a block away from the ballpark.

• "Clubhouse chemistry" refers to how well the team gets along with one another, on and off the field. One of the classic questions in baseball, akin to "which came first, the chicken or the egg?" is the riddle of whether consistent winning breeds positive chemistry or whether positive chemistry breeds consistent winning. Whatever tact one takes, numerous exceptions to the rule have survived the decades, either in positive chemistry/last place clubs or first place teams that can't stand one another.

• After a game, there is a set time period for "cooling off" before the assembled media members are allowed to stream in and conduct their interviews.

• A "clubhouse lawyer" is a player given to expressing his opinions loudly and at great length, particularly with regard to complaints. Or, as Joe Garagiola put it in *Sport* magazine in 1962, "A clubhouse lawyer is .210 hitter who isn't playing. He gripes about everything. His locker is too near the dryer. His shoes aren't ever shined right. His undershirt isn't dry. His bats don't have the good knots in them that the stars' bats have. He's not playing because the manager is dumb. When he does play he says, 'Well, what could you expect? I ain't played in two weeks.' And he's a perpetual second guesser."

• As the baseball adage goes, "What happens in the clubhouse stays in the clubhouse."

"In the Milwaukee clubhouse there's a sign that reads: 'What you say here, what you see here, what you do here and what you hear here, let it stay here.' The same sign hangs in the clubhouse in Minneapolis. Also, I suppose, in the CIA offices in Washington. If I were a CIA man, could I write a book?"

– Jim Bouton, *Ball Four*

clubhouse attendant
n. clubbie, clubby; SPECIFIC clubhouse boy, clubhouse man, clubhouse manager

"The clubhouse dues in the minors are $10 a day. Up here, it's $50 a day, $60 a day. There literally is major league inflation."

– Twins third baseman Danny Valencia, *St. Paul Pioneer*

Press; June 23, 2011

crowd
n. assemblage, assembly, attendance, congregation, crush, devoted, drove, faithful, fans, gathering, hopeful, mass, masses, mob, multitude, rooters, stadium, throng; SPANISH fanáticos, multitúd

"Take me out to the ballgame/Take me out with the crowd..."
– "Take Me Out to the Ballgame," written by 29-year-old Jack Norworth, 1908

• boo
v. berate, blast, deride, heckle, hiss, hoot, jeer, razz, root against, voice one's distaste

• A "Bronx cheer" may be a raspberry, the contemptuous sound made by sticking the tongue between the lips and blowing, or a sarcastic cheer accorded an umpire, manager, or player. A pitcher who has thrown 10 straight pitches outside of the strike zone might well receive a Bronx cheer for his next called strike.

• A controversial play or player/umpire's actions may aggravate, agitate, anger, bait, chafe, displease, egg on, enrage, gall, goad, incense, incite, inflame, infuriate, instigate, madden, miff, nettle, provoke, rankle, rile, rile up, stir up, or work the home crowd into a lather.

"You're trying your damnedest, you strike out and they boo you. I act like it doesn't bother me, like I don't hear anything the fans say, but the truth is I hear every word of it and it kills me."
– Hall of Famer Mike Schmidt (1972-1989)

• **cheer**
v. acclaim, applaud, appreciate, approve, commend, give a hand, give an ovation, hail, laud, praise, rave, root for, salute, support

• An outstanding play may amaze, arouse, astonish, astound, awaken, awe, catalyze, delight, dynamize, electrify, energize, excite, fire up, galvanize, lift, rev up, rouse, thrill, wake up, or wow the crowd.

• A positively roaring crowd, overjoyed with the game's latest turn of events, is said to be "going wild."

• A "curtain call" occurs when a crowd's jubilant cheers cause a player to re-emerge from the dugout, acknowledging their approval perhaps with a tip/wave of his cap. As Peter Morris writes in *A Game of Inches,* "during Detroit's first major league game in 1881, the *Detroit Free Press* reported that Charley Bennett hit a home run that was 'loudly applauded, and the crowd would not desist until he bowed in acknowledgment' (*Detroit Free Press,* May 3, 1881)."

"When 20,000 people applaud as you walk out to do your job, it should be an inspiration."
– Jim Brosnan, *The Long Season*

• **make noise**
n. bark, bellow, bluster, clamor, cry out, holler, howl, raise a ruckus, roar, scream, screech, shout, shriek, yell

curve/curveball
n. around the horn, Aunt Susie, barrel-hoop, bender, breaker, buckler, bulge, cement-mixer, corkscrew/corkscrew-er, corkscrew twist, cow's horn,

crook, crooked pitch, deuce, dewdrop, dinky-doo, dipsy-doodle, downer, downshoot, equalizer, fast-breaker, fish, fish hook, hammer, helicopter, hipper-dipper, hook, hoopdy-scoop, inner-outer, jug, jughandle, knee-buckler, mystifier, number two (or #2), offshoot, Old Sal, pretzel, public enemy #1, rainbow, shoot, slant, snake, snapper (or Mr. Snappy), swerve, twist, upper-downer, whirler, yakker, yellow hammer, zigzagger; SPECIFIC drop curve, inshoot, hanger, hanging curve, knuckle-curve, lollipop, Lord Charles, out-curve, out drop, outshoot, roundhouse, short curve, slow-breaker, slow curve, snapdragon, snapper, spinner, Uncle Charlie; SPANISH curva

• **pitch a curveball**
v. balloon, bend, break, break off, bulge, corkscrew, drop, float, put a wrinkle in it, slice, snap, snap off, snapdragon, spin, twist

• William Arthur "Candy" Cummings (1872-1877) was elected to the Hall of Fame in 1939 for the sole reason that he was believed to have invented the curveball. The claim is highly questionable. Writes Rob Neyer in *The Neyer/James Guide to Pitchers*, "Of course, others have been credited with inventing the curveball, most notably Bobby Matthews (who's also been described as the inventor of both the fadeaway/screwball and the spitball; a clever lad, he must have been), but also Phonie Martin, Fred Goldsmith, Terry Larkin, and at least a few more."

• A curveball is often described compared to the numbers on an analog clock. A 12-to-6 curve has straight "north to south" movement, for example, while an 11-to-5 curve has somewhat more of a diagonally dropping path.

• When a catcher signals which pitch to throw, a fastball is indicated by one finger while a curveball is indicated by two fingers. Hence, the fastball is nicknamed "#1" while the curve is nicknamed "#2." (A pitcher's third pitch, usually the change-up, is indicated by three fingers. A pickoff throw is generally indicated with a fist, no fingers showing.)

• A weak curve is a "lollipop" or a "hanger." A hanging curveball does not have sharp downward movement, allowing the batter to hit it with ease.

• A well-thrown curveball with sharp breaking action is called cruel, dirty, filthy, nasty, vicious, or wicked.

• "Uncle Charlie" is a complimentary name for an excellent curveball. When Dwight Gooden (1984-2000) first arrived in the National League, his curve was so dynamic that it was clear "Uncle Charlie" wasn't high enough praise. Instead, Gooden's curve was known as "Sir Charles."

D

Clarence "Pants" Rowland, manager of the Chicago White Sox, (right) talks with his pitcher, Eddie Cicotte (left) in the dugout during a game.
(Courtesy Library of Congress, LC-USZ62-133664.)

defeat

n. see *loss*

v. ace, annex, arrest, attend to, avenge, bag, beat, best, better, block, breeze, bump, cage, can, cap, check, chop down, circumvent, clear, coast, cop, crown, cruise, curb, cut down, cut off, daunt, deflate, deny, derail, disappoint, dish, dismiss, deal a loss, deep six, discard, dispatch, dispose of, dodge, do in, double up, douse, down, drop, dump, ease, eclipse, exceed, fell, finish off, fly past, foil, get by, get past, get to, give the boot, halt, hand a loss, hang ten (for a ten-run output or a tenth straight win), harpoon, haunt, head off, hose, hurdle, jackknife, jar, knock, leap, leapfrog, lift, nettle, nonplus, notch, oust, outclass, outgun, outhit, outmuscle, outpace, outrun, outscore, outslug, outstrip, overcome, overstep, overtake, pass, pick on, pin, pin down, plug, polish off, pop, post (a win), prevail over, pull away from, put away, quash, quell, rattle, raze, rebuff, reel in, reject, repel, repulse, resist, rise above, ruffle, sack, sail, scale, scuttle, shoot down, sink, slay, solve, spill, spoil, stagger, stop, submarine, surmount, surpass, swindle, tag, take, take care of, take down, tame, thwart, tie up, top, topple, trip, trip up, triumph over, trump, turn back, unhinge, unplug, upend, upset, vault past, vanquish, veto, victimize, ward off, wear down, wing, zap

• A losing team with an animal nickname may be "tamed" or "caged" while a losing team with an aerial nickname may be "grounded."

• A key player may bring, carry, catapult, drive, elevate, launch, lift, power, send, or shoot his team past the opposition.

• **defeat convincingly, soundly, or by a wide margin**

v. annihilate, ash, assail, assault, awe, barrel over, bash, batter, beat down, beat up, belt, blast, blister, blow away, blow out, bludgeon, bomb, bombard, bowl over, brain, bulldoze, bully, bumrush, burn, bury, bust, butcher, buzzsaw, carve up, claw, claw apart, clean their clocks, clean up, clobber, clock, club, conk, conquer, cream, crush, dazzle, decimate, deck, demolish, dent, destroy, devastate, devour, dice up, dismantle, dominate, drill, drown, drub, drum, dust, embarrass, eviscerate, explode, expose, flatten, flog, gang up on, gash, gut, hammer, handle, house, humble, humiliate, jolt, jump on, kill, knock around, knock out, K-O (or K.O.), ladle, lambaste, laminate, leather, level, lick, light up, manhandle, massacre, mash, maul, mow down, murder, obliterate, overpower, overrun, overwhelm, paddle, paste, plant, plaster, poleax, pounce on, pound, powder, power past, pulverize, pummel, punish, quash, race past, ram, ravage, rip, rock, roll, romp, rough up, rout, rule, run away from, run over, run roughshod over, scalp, school, shame, shell, shellack, shred, skin, slam, slaughter, smack, smack down, smash, smear, smite, smoke, snuff, spank, spike, squash, squelch, stampede, steamroll, stomp, stuff, swallow, swamp, swarm, swat, take apart, take to the cleaners, take their lunch money, tan, tattoo, tear apart, tear down, tear into, thrash, throttle, thump, thunder, torch, total, trample, trash, trounce, wallop, waste, wax, whack, whale on, whip, whomp, whop, whup, wipe out, work over, wreck, zip over, zip past

• An easy win is a blowout, cakewalk, laugher, party, romp, rout, or walkover.

• **defeat by a smaller margin**
v. clip, edge, eke out, escape, nick, nip, nose out, pull out, shade, shave, slip by/past, sneak by/past, squeak out/past, squeeze, tip, tiptoe by/past, trim

• **defeat via shutout**
v. blank, Chicago, hold scoreless, schneider, shut out,

skunk, whitewash, zip; SPANISH blanquear

• **defeat in extra innings**
v. go the distance, outbattle, outlast, persevere, persist

• **defeat due to outstanding pitching**
v. baffle, bottle up, confound, confuse, contain, daze, dazzle, flabbergast, flummox, fluster, frustrate, gag, handcuff, hogtie, hold down, master, mesmerize, muffle, muzzle, mystify, neutralize, outduel, outpitch, perplex, puzzle, quiet, riddle, shackle, shut down, silence, smother, stifle, stump, stymie, subdue, suffocate, suppress

• **defeat due to a comeback**
v. catch, come from behind, rally past, steal, sting, swipe

• **defeat after withstanding an opponent's best efforts**
v. fend off, fight off, hold at bay, hold off, hold on, stave off, survive

• **defeat a favored opponent unexpectedly**
v. ambush, jolt, shock, startle, stun, surprise, upset, waylay

double
n. double bagger, keystone hit, two-bagger, two-base hit, two-baser, two-cushion shot, two-sacker; SPECIFIC automatic double, ground-rule double, hustle double, rule-book double; SPANISH biangular, doble, tubey

• A ground-rule double, also called an automatic double or a rule-book double, is a double awarded due to a special circumstance outlined in the stadium's ground rules, such as when a fair batted ball bounces out of the field of play or is touched by a reaching fan. A ground-rule double is also awarded at Wrigley Field if a batter hits a ball into the ivy hanging on the wall and the outfielder immediately throws his hands in the air, giving up on the play rather than attempting to find the ball.

• A hustle double occurs when a batter hits what looks to be a single but makes his way to second base safely through daring and speed.

• The career Major League leader in doubles is the "Grey Eagle," Hall of Famer Tris Speaker (1907-1928), who collected 792 two-baggers in his career. Speaker had five different seasons with at least 50 doubles, including a 52-double season in 1926 when he was 38-years-old.

• The single-season record for doubles was enjoyed by a more anonymous individual, Red Sox right-fielder Earl Webb (1925, 1927-1928, 1930-1933). In 1931, Webb cranked 67 doubles, 20 more than any other player in the Majors. It was a spectacular accomplishment, but Webb did not exactly build upon the success. In the rest of his seven-year career, he had only 88 doubles.

doubleheader
n. bargain bill, doubledip, twin bill, twinbill; SPANISH doble juego

• **doubleheader, win one game**
v. halve, split

• **doubleheader, win both games**
v. break out the brooms, double up, sweep

• A doubleheader refers to two games played in the same ballpark between the same teams on the same day.

• There are notable exceptions. The Mets and Yankees battled in home-and-home doubleheaders in 2000, 2003, and 2008, playing one game at the Mets' former home of Shea Stadium and the other at old Yankee Stadium. On September 25, 2000, the Cleveland Indians played a home doubleheader against two different opponents, making up a previous rainout with a Game 1 matchup vs. the Chicago White Sox (an Indians 9-2 win) before taking on the Minnesota Twins in Game 2 (a 4-3 Cleveland loss).

• Doubleheaders used to be scheduled in advance, particularly on Sundays and holidays. Currently, to the displeasure of the nostalgic fan, doubleheaders are only held to make up a prior rainout or postponement.

• Game 1 of a doubleheader is the "opener" or the "curtain raiser."

• Game 2 of a doubleheader is the "nightcap."

• A day-night doubleheader requires separate tickets for each game, one in the afternoon and one in the evening.

• A twi-night doubleheader (or "twi-nighter") is a doubleheader played entirely at night.

• A "double-barreled matinee" is played in the afternoon.

• A relative to the double-barreled matinee, the "classic" doubleheader sees Game 1 played in the early afternoon and Game 2 played slightly later in the day but before evening can set in.

• "High mass" refers to a Sunday doubleheader.

• There have been three tripleheaders in Major League

history, featuring three full games in one day: Brooklyn vs. Pittsburgh on September 1, 1890; Baltimore vs. Louisville on September 7, 1896; and Pittsburgh vs. Cincinnati on October 2, 1920.

"Let's play two."
– Hall of Famer Ernie Banks (1953-1971)

double play
n. Al Capone, deuce, DP, double, double killing, doublet, pitcher's best friend, twin killing, two-ply killing; SPANISH doble jugada, doble matanza

• A double play is commonly described based on the scoring of the defensive players involved. The scoring of defensive players, first laid out by 19th century pioneer Henry Chadwick, is as follows: pitcher (1), catcher (2), first baseman (3), second baseman (4), third baseman (5), shortstop (6), left fielder (7), center fielder (8), right fielder (9). A double play that goes from the shortstop to the second baseman to the first baseman is considered a "6-4-3" double play.

• When defensive players complete a double play, they "turn two" or "get two for the price of one."

• The exciting action of a "strike 'em out, throw 'em out double play" sees the pitcher complete a strikeout followed by the catcher throwing out an attempted basestealer.

• An "unassisted double play" occurs when both outs are recorded by the same player.

• A "reverse force" double play occurs when a force play is recorded for the first out, removing all subsequent force plays and forcing the second out to be recorded via tag.

• Infamous gangster Al Capone became dubiously linked with double plays thanks to the common double-play nickname of "twin killing."

• On April 23, 2011, the Lansing Lugnuts and West Michigan Whitecaps combined for a record-setting 10 double plays in nine innings. Whitecaps catcher Rob Brantly fittingly ended the game by lining into West Michigan's sixth double play of the game, handled in unassisted fashion by first baseman K.C. Hobson to conclude a 6-1 Lansing win.

• The Brooklyn Dodgers' Babe Herman (1926-1937, 1945) is credited, according to legend, with tripling into a triple play on August 15, 1926. That's not exactly true; he merely doubled into a double play. Herman came to the plate with the bases loaded and belted one off the wall in right field. From third base, runner Hank DeBerry scored with ease. From second base, Dodgers pitcher Dazzy Vance cautiously approached third and turned hopefully toward home plate before having second thoughts. He returned to third base – at the very same time as the runner from first base, Chick Fewster, arrived. Shortly thereafter, the Babe himself blindly stampeded into the bag. The Boston catcher applied tags all around, with Herman and Fewster each ruled out on the play. The Dodgers did win the game, 4-1, part of a doubleheader sweep for Brooklyn.

"The poet or storyteller who feels that he is competing with a superb double play in the World Series is a lost man. One would not want as a reader a man who did not appreciate the finesse of a double play."

– acclaimed author John Cheever

dugout

n. coop, dog kennel, hole, kennel, pit; SPANISH cueva

• There is no specific designation in the rule book as to whether the home team receives the first-base side or third-base side dugout. The choice is up to the home team.

• Before dugouts, players would sit on an open bench to each side of the field. It is believed that dugouts were first created, thanks to digging out an area below the surface for each team to make its headquarters, in order to allow fans to better see the field.

• The longtime Florida State League team in Vero Beach, also the longtime Spring Training home of the Los Angeles Dodgers, only had a bench to represent its dugout. There was no shelter or roof to shield players from the sun.

• The bench in the dugout is also known as the "pine" since it was commonly made of pine wood.

• A player who doesn't start is said to "ride the bench" or "ride the pine."

E

Billy Shindle of the Baltimore Orioles. Yes, the baseball card misspells the name.
(Courtesy Library of Congress, LC-DIG-bbc-0405f.)

error

n. blunder, bobble, bonehead play, boner, boot, botch, bungle, butter, clinker, drop, E, faux pas, flub, fluff, foozle, foul-up, fozzle, fumble, gift, gaffe, goof, goof-up, howler, juggle, kick, lapse, mess-up, miscue, misfortune, mishandling, miscalculation, misjudgment, misplay, misstep, mistake, muff, muffed ball, rock, screw-up, sin, slip-up, transgression; SPECIFIC fielding error, three-base error, throwing error, two-base error; SPANISH error

• An error is referred to with regard to how many bases it allows the opposition. A three-base error allows the batter to reach third base while scoring a runner from first base.

• error, commit an

v. blow, bobble, boot, botch, bungle, butcher, drop, flub, fluff, fumble, goof, juggle, kick, lose in the sun (or the lights), make a mess of, mess up, miscalculate, mishandle, misjudge, misplay, muff, mug, screw up

• A fielder "fights the ball" when he reaches for the ball before it arrives.

• A ball that is misplayed off of a tough hop is said to have "handcuffed" or "eaten up" the fielder, who could not "find the handle."

• The record for most errors committed in a season is an improbable 122 errors, held by the infielders Herman Long (1889-1904) and Billy Shindle (1886-1898). Long set the original mark in 1889, making 117 miscues at shortstop and five more at second base. This was no anomalous season, either; Long struggled to a Major League record 1,096 errors in his career.

• Billy Shindle had been a third baseman from 1887-1889

before moving to shortstop in 1890 in the short-lived Player's League and turning it into a disaster area (though it should be mentioned that he was an offensive superstar with 21 doubles, 21 triples, 10 home runs and a league-leading 282 total bases). Shindle moved right back to third base in the National League in 1891 and committed "only" 58 errors in 103 games.

• Comparatively, over the past three decades only the immortal Jose Offerman has been able to pile up 40 or more errors in a season. The 23-year-old Offerman made 42 errors at shortstop for the Dodgers in 1992.

"In football, you receive a penalty. In baseball, you make an error."
– comedian George Carlin, "Baseball and Football"

extra innings
n. bonus baseball, extra baseball, extras, free baseball; SPANISH innings extra

• Any other synonym for "innings" (such as "frames") may be inserted after bonus, extra, or free, i.e. 'bonus frames.' See *innings* for options.

• A notably drawn-out game, whether due to excessive innings or duration, is called a "marathon."

• In American professional baseball, if a game is tied after nine innings, the two teams will continue to play one inning at a time until a winner is decided or curfew is reached. In Japanese professional baseball, 12 innings is a game's maximum length. If the two teams are deadlocked at the end of 12, a tie is recorded.

• The International Baseball Federation uses a "reboot" system once the game reaches the 11th inning, placing a player at second base at the start of an at-bat in the hopes of encouraging a run-scoring rally.

• If a game reaches the 14th inning, the home crowd is likely to hold a second 7th-inning stretch, re-singing "Take Me Out to the Ballgame."

• A "single-game doubleheader" is an extra-inning game that takes 18 innings to complete, equal to two nine-inning games.

• The longest extra-inning game in Major League history was played on May 1, 1920, between the Brooklyn Robins (later the Dodgers) and the Boston Braves. Respective starting pitchers Leon Cadore and Joe Oeschger each went the entire 26 innings of the 1-1 tie. Brooklyn tallied its run off of Oeschger in the fifth inning; Boston answered against Cadore in the bottom of the sixth. Twenty scoreless frames followed before the game was called. Each pitcher struck out seven batters; Oeschger allowed nine base hits while Cadore was reached for 15 safeties. In all, Major League Baseball's longest contest took only three hours and 50 minutes to play. Brooklyn went on to win the National League pennant before losing the World Series to Cleveland.

• On April 18, 1981, the Triple-A International League's Rochester Red Wings, with future Hall of Famer Cal Ripken, Jr. (1981-2001), took on the Pawtucket Red Sox, with future Hall of Famer Wade Boggs (1982-1999). Things nearly ended nice and early, but Pawtucket's Russ Laribee provided a sacrifice fly in the bottom of the ninth to spoil Rochester starter Larry Jones' shutout bid and force a surplus of extra innings. The teams exchanged runs in the

21st inning and played onward, deeper into the night. By 3 a.m., the clubs were burning parts of the bench in the dugout and broken bats in the bullpen in order to stay warm. At last, under the orders of just-woken-up International League President Harold Cooper, they called it a night at the end of the 32nd inning. The score was still tied at 2-2; it was just past 4 a.m. The game concluded two months later on June 23, requiring only 18 anticlimactic minutes before Pawtucket's Dave Koza provided an RBI single to win the game, 3-2, in 33 innings. In all, the game required over 800 pitches and lasted eight hours and 25 minutes.

"We're getting better. It's taking them longer to beat us."
– Hall of Fame manager Casey Stengel, after an extra-innings defeat

F

New York City fans at 7:00 a.m., outside the Polo Grounds. *(Courtesy Library of Congress, LC-DIG-ppmsca-18461.)*

fan

n. ant, apologist, ballite, baseballeer, baseballite, bug, crank, devotee, diamond bug, diehard, fanatic, filbert, krank, nut, partisan, patron, rooter, turnstiler; SPECIFIC baseball widow, baseball widower, bleacher bum, bleacher creature, bleacherite, crankess, crankette, dyed-in-the-wool fan, fly, front runner, gate crasher, grandstander, grandstand manager, hooter, John fan, knot-hole customer, kranklet, leather lungs, lifer, luxury box Larry, newbie, pest, pink hat, plugger, purist, seamhead, stathead, walk-up customer, wolf; SPANISH fanático

• Created by the Oakland Raiders and popularized by the Ohio State Buckeyes and the Boston Red Sox, each fanbase may now also be considered a “Nation.”

• The term “ant” derives from the player’s point-of-view, where the fans in the stands can look as tiny as ants.

• A “baseball widow” (or “baseball widower,” for that matter) is a non-fan whose spouse’s love of baseball during the season causes her/him to feel neglected.

• An angry fan is a “bleacher critic” or “boo bird.” A group of angry fans comprise an “anvil chorus.”

• A fan who loves the team’s manager is a “bobo.”

• A fan who only roots for a team during successful seasons is a “fair-weather” fan, or “climbing on the bandwagon.”

• A fan who only cares about a winning team is a “front runner.”

• A woman who has a weakness for baseball players is considered a “green fly,” a “Baseball Annie,” or a “Baseball Sadie,” and is often referred to by the players as “beef” or a “cleat-chaser.”

• The “Bleacher Bums” are a group of hardcore Chicago Cubs fans, formed in 1966, who root faithfully for their beloved team from the bleachers of Wrigley Field.

• The “Bleacher Creatures” used to be the fans in the center field bleachers at Tiger Stadium, who caused havoc and controversy with their actions and language in the 1970s and 1980s. The current “Bleacher Creatures” are the fiercely loyal and exuberantly raucous Yankees fans who previously sat in Sections 37 and 39 at old Yankee Stadium and now make their habitat in Section 203 in the right-field bleachers at the new Yankee Stadium. The Yanks' Bleacher Creatures are best known for their "roll call" occurring before the first pitch of each home game, chanting the name of each New York outfielder and infielder until he acknowledges them with a point, a tip of the cap, or, in the case of Nick Swisher, a full-on salute.

• "Rooters Row" was one of the early 20th century forerunners of the Bleacher Creatures, a rowdy (and inebriated) group of Reds faithful at their gloriously named "Palace of the Fans" (1902-1911). At the same time, there was a pocket of Boston Red Sox fans known proudly as the "Royal Rooters."

• A "seamhead" or "stathead" is a baseball fan who cares about statistics and what they reveal about players and tactics. Such a fan may consider himself/herself a sabermetrician or sabrmetrician. Sabermetrics is the distinct study of baseball statistics, a term coined by Bill James deriving from SABR (the Society of American Baseball Research, pronounced *sabre*, and concerned with every aspect of the game's history).

"An ardent supporter of the home town team should go to a game prepared to take offense, no matter what happens."
– humorist Robert Benchley

fastball
n. alto queso, aspirin tablet, bat messer, blazer, breezer, bump, burner, buzzer, cannon shot, cheddar, cheese, dark one, dart, dead red, express, fireball, flameball, fog, fogger, gas, gas face, good cheese, good express, hard ball, hard cheese, hard one, heat, heater, high cheese, high hard one, hot rock, hummer, Linda Ronstadt, Louisiana, low lead, mustard, number one (or #1), pitch with mustard/tabasco on

it, popcorn, powder, red-ball express, scorcher, sizzler, smoke, smokeball, smoker, soaker, speedball, steam, steamer, swift, swift ball, swifty, terminator, whistler, whiz-bang, yakker; SPECIFIC batting-practice fastball, chainsaw, cross-seamer, cross-seam fastball, cut fastball, cutter, darting hummer, four-seamer, four-seam fastball, hopper, jammer, jump ball, keyhole fastball, little ball, muscle heat, Peggy Lee fastball, pitch of the 1980s, pneumonia ball, radio ball, radio pitch, riding fastball, riser, rising fastball, room-service cheeseburger, sailer, short fastball, sinking fastball, small baseball, sneaker, split-fingered fastball, splitter, two-seamer, two-seam fastball; SPANISH bola rápida, recta

"No matter how fast a fastball travels, someone, somehow, will catch up to it."
– Paul Dickson, *The Unwritten Rules of Baseball*

• **pitch a fastball**
v. blaze, bring it, burn, bury, challenge, cut, dart, drill, fire, flame, fog, give (or show) the gas face, hum, pop the mitt, pour, powder, power, ride, rifle, scorch, sizzle, smoke, speed, steam, whistle, zip

• **pitch a cut fastball** ("chainsaw" or "cutter")
v. bite, bore, cut, gnaw, run (to the inside or outside)

• A four-seam fastball (four-seamer or cross-seamer) is held across the seams and comes in straight and hard.

• A two-seam fastball (two-seamer) is held along the seams and arrives with less velocity but more movement (sinking or tailing) than a four-seam fastball.

• *Alto queso* is Spanish for "high cheese."

• "Linda Ronstadt" is a punnish reference related to Ronstadt's "Blue Bayou" album, as in "That fastball blew by you." Likewise, "Louisiana" is noted for its bayous.

• A "radio ball" can only be heard, not seen.

• A "pneumonia ball" is so fast, a batter could catch pneumonia from the chilly wind stirred up by its passing.

• Attributed to Tug McGraw (1965-1984), a "Peggy Lee fastball" is slower than expected, referencing Miss Peggy Lee's 1969 song "Is That All There is?"

• A pitcher known for his fastball is a fireballer, flame-thrower, or power pitcher.

• The opposite of a power pitcher is a finesse pitcher (a "sharpshooter" or "dabber"), who makes his living with "junk" or "slop."

• A fastball thrown especially hard has cheese, giddy-up, hot sauce, mustard, salsa, stink, or Tabasco on it.

• A fastball with great movement may be said to be alive, live, or lively, and may "hop" or "jump" due to its "late life."

• "Sit" is used to refer to both a pitcher's constant velocity ("He's sitting at 92 miles-per-hour") and when a batter expects a pitch ("He's sitting on the fastball"). A batter who is expecting a fastball can also be said to be "sitting dead red."

• In the 1940s, it's said that Cleveland Indians Hall of Famer Bob Feller (1936-1941, 1945-1956) had his fastball timed at 107.6 miles-per-hour by military equipment.

• On September 24, 2010, 22-year-old Cincinnati Reds left-hander Aroldis Chapman fired a pitch that clocked in at 105.1 miles-per-hour.

"The pitcher has to find out if the hitter is timid. And if the hitter is timid, he has to remind the hitter he's timid."
– Hall of Famer Don Drysdale (1956-1969); July 9, 1979, in the *New York Times*

fielder
n. defender, gloveman, glovesman; SPANISH fildeador

fight
n. altercation, battle royal/royale, brannigan, brawl, brouhaha, donnybrook, dustup, fracas, fray, free-for-all, melee, rhubarb, rumble, rumpus, scrap, scuffle, shindig, skirmish; SPANISH pelea

• A fight touched off by multiple hit batsmen is a "beanbrawl."

• A bench-clearing brawl sees both dugouts empty onto the field to support their teammates. Such a brawl is likely to involve both bullpens, too, with the opposing relievers running side by side into the fray before turning against one another.

"Baseball fights are to fighting what artificial turf is to grass – it looks like a fight and sounds like a fight, but it isn't really a fight."
– umpire Ron Luciano

first base
n. corner, first, first sack, gateway, getaway bag, initial bag, initial corner, initial cushion, initial hassock, initial sack; SPANISH primera base

fly ball
n. air ball, balloon, balloon flier, big league fly, cloud-buster, cloud-hunter, cloud-scraper, cloud-searcher, drive, fly, fungo, high fly, palomita, rain-bringer, second-story drive, skyscraper, towering fly; SPANISH fly

• hit a fly ball
v. boost, catapult, elevate, fly, get under, hoist, launch, lift, lot, pop, raise, send upward, sky, uppercut

• The flight of a fly ball is described by how it carries, usually due to weather conditions such as humidity or wind. A fly ball that "carries well" travels farther than expected. A fly ball that "carries poorly" travels shallower than expected.

• A routine fly ball is considered "drifting," "easy," or "lazy."

• An easy flyout for an outfielder is a "can of corn" (also called "popcorn"). It is also said that an easy fly ball could be caught in an outfielder's "hip pocket" or "back pocket."

• A fly ball hit directly at an outfielder means he "doesn't have to move a muscle." In such a play, the outfielder is given credit for perfect defensive positioning (or having the batter "played perfectly").

fly ball landing softly between infield and outfield

n. awful, banjo, banjo hit, batazo podrido, bleeder, bloop, blooper, chinker, dipper, drooper, dropper, dunker, duck fart, duck snort, dying quail, dying swan, fister, flare, grenade, half-liner, hand grenade, humpback liner, jam-shot, lazy fly, lazy hit, leaping Lena, lollipop, looper, nubber, parachute, percentage hit, plunker, pooper, pop fly, punker, seagull, sinker, smell hit, special, squib, squirrel, stinker, sucker, Texas Leaguer, Texas Leaguer fly, Texas Leaguer hit, tuberculosis liner, tweener, up-over; SPANISH ñameado

• **hit a fly ball softly between the infield and outfield**
v. bloop, dip, droop, drop, dump, dunk, flare, floop, loop, plunk

foul ball
n. cackler, cackle clout, foul, hen-house hoist

• **foul ball, hit a**
v. clip, deflect, fight off, foul back, foul off, get a piece of, hang in, send aside, send backward, spoil, stay alive, tip

• A batter who fouls a pitch off to avoid striking out is "guarding the plate," "protecting the plate," or "staying alive."

• A batter who fouls a ball straight back "just missed it."

• A batter who fouls off several pitches is told to "straighten it out."

• A deep fly ball or home run that barely lands foul is a long strike or a loud foul (or any combination of the two).

• In early baseball, there used to such a thing as a "fairfoul" hit, where a ball would be ruled fair if it started out in fair territory before rolling foul. Ross Barnes (1871-1877, 1879, 1881) took advantage of the rule to purposely bunt the ball from fair ground into foul ground, beating out easy hits and compiling a batting average above .400. In modern baseball, a ball must end up in fair territory in order to be ruled a fair ball. A line drive that bounces back from the pitcher's mound toward home plate and is picked up in foul ground is a foul ball. Meanwhile a grounder that starts off foul toward one of the dugouts but takes a funny hop back into fair ground is a fair ball.

• As 1981 Mariners third basemen Lenny Randle and 1987 Royals third baseman Kevin Seitzer each discovered, it is illegal to re-direct a slow roller up the line into foul territory by blowing upon it, no matter how creative the idea or how hilarious the sight.

• The ability of Hall of Fame shortstop Luke Appling (1930-1943, 1945-1950) to willfully produce foul balls while waiting for a good pitch to hit – or for other purposes – was famous in his day and for generations afterward. One story tells of White Sox ownership's refusal to grant baseballs to fans for autographs and/or souvenirs, reasoning that the balls were far too expensive to give away. Appling responded with a slew of foul balls in game after game until ownership relented. Another tale saw Appling slowly but surely wear away at Yankees Hall of Fame pitcher Red Ruffing with foul after foul until the frustrated and tiring Ruffing gave in and was knocked out of the game shortly thereafter.

foul line
n. boundary, chalk, line

• As has been noted wryly by numerous baseball wags, both the foul line and foul pole are technically in fair territory. A batted ball that lands on any part of the foul line beyond first or third base is considered fair while a batted ball that hits the foul pole is considered a home run. With this in mind, a number of broadcasters have taken it upon themselves to use the term "fair pole." This seemed to bother former MLB manager Bobby Bragan; when Fort Worth's LaGrave Field was rebuilt in 2002, the Fort Worth Cats installed "fair poles" down each line on his advice.

foul territory
n. foul ground, out of play; ANTONYM fair territory, in play

front office
n. biggies, brain trust, brass, execs, executives, management, men upstairs, suits, top brass, upper management; SPECIFIC assistant general manager, assistant to the general manager, chairman, chief executive officer (CEO), chief operating officer (COO), director, general manager (GM), owner, president, principal owner, special assistant to the general manager, vice chairman, vice president; SPANISH oficina principal

• The front office personnel is generally concerned more with the business side of the franchise, the bottom line of team performance, and public/media relations rather than the nuts and bolts of the baseball side. There have been exceptions. Hall of Famer Cornelius McGillicuddy, more familiarly known as Connie Mack (1894-1896, 1901-1950), doubled as the owner and manager of the Philadelphia Athletics.

• In 1977, Atlanta Braves owner Ted Turner decided to take

a turn as manager, sending Dave Bristol off "on assignment" and skippering the Braves for a game. Atlanta lost, and National League President Chub Feeney ordered Turner back to the owner's box immediately thereafter.

"Managing isn't that difficult. You just have to score more runs than the other guy."

– Braves owner Ted Turner (1976-1996)

G

The grounds crew preps home plate before the game.
(Courtesy Library of Congress, LC-DIG-ggbain-10111.)

game
n. affair, battle, bill, bout, contest, duel, encounter, journey, match-up/matchup, meeting, outing, struggle, tilt; SPECIFIC curtain-jerker, matinee, night game, opener, rubber game/match; SPANISH juego

• A low-scoring game is a "pitcher's duel."

• A high-scoring game is a "slugfest."

• game, close
n. anyone's game, barnburner, nail-biter, nip and tuck,

seesaw, thriller, tight one

• A close game goes "back and forth" and "down to the wire" and may very well turn out to be an "instant classic."

• A "rollercoaster" game features many twists, turns, lead changes, and momentum shifts.

"The game was closer than the score indicated."
– Hall of Famer Dizzy Dean (1930, 1932-1941, 1947) on a 1-0 game, *Men at Work*

"It ain't over till it's over."
– Hall of Famer Lawrence "Yogi" Berra (1946-1963, 1965)

glove
n. leather, mitt; SPECIFIC basket glove, Big Bertha, board, bushel basket, catcher's mitt, D&M glove, eagle claw, first baseman's mitt, fishnet, gamer, H glove, iron glove, lead glove, lobster net, lobster trap, orange crate, pad, pancake, pillow, pud, rag, skillet, tenney, thimble, tin glove, trapper's mitt; SPANISH guante

• The word "mitt," once used interchangeably with "glove," is now mostly reserved for describing a larger glove, such as a catcher's mitt or first baseman's mitt.

• "Board," "iron glove," "lead glove," and "skillet" refer to the glove of a poor defensive player.

• Dick Stuart (1958-1966, 1969) slammed 66 home runs in the Class A Western League in 1956 and went on to slug 228 homers and receive three All-Star honors in the Major Leagues. But Stuart gained wider notoriety, as well as the nicknames "Dr. Strangeglove" and "Stonefingers" (among others), for his notoriously poor fielding skills at first base. The story is told of the time that Stuart received a standing ovation for cleanly snagging a windblown hot dog wrapper. The big first baseman went so far as to order a license plate that read "E-3" (an official scorer's designation of an error on a first baseman).

"I know I'm the world's worst fielder, but who gets paid for fielding? There isn't a great fielder in all of baseball getting the kind of dough I get for hitting."

– Dick Stuart

grand slam
n. demolition derby, four aces, grand salami, grand slammer, grannie, jackpot, salami, slammer; SPANISH jonrón con bases llena

• The term "grand slam" comes from contract bridge. It refers to a side making level 7 and taking all 13 tricks.

"Get out the rye bread and mustard, Grandma, it's grand salami time!"

– Dave Niehaus, voice of the Seattle Mariners

ground ball, bouncing
n. bouncer, bounder, chopper, grass disturber, grasshopper, grounder, hopper, skipper; SPECIFIC alabaster blast, alabaster blaster, Baltimore Chop, dirter, grasser, Pittsburgh chopper; SPANISH roletazo, rolin

• A "dirter" is hit on the infield dirt while a "grasser" is hit on the infield grass.

• An "alabaster blast" (or blaster) is a term coined by

Pittsburgh Pirates broadcaster Bob Prince with regard to the high chopping base hits off of the hard Forbes Field infield, also known as a "Pittsburgh chopper."

• A "Baltimore Chop" is a bouncer hit extraordinarily high in front of home plate. It refers to the 19th century Baltimore Orioles, who had their groundskeeper harden the area in front of the plate. The Orioles then gained easy hits by purposefully chopping the ball into the hard ground.

• **hit a bouncing ground ball**
v. bounce, bound, butcher-boy, Baltimore Chop, chop, ground, skip, splash, tomahawk

• A batter using a "butcher-boy" or "tomahawk" stroke swings sharply downward with his bat, purposefully hitting the ball on the ground.

• **easy bounce to field**, caused by a smooth infield
n. Big Bill (grabbed when the ball is as high as the bill of the fielder's baseball cap), charity hop, easy hop, good hop, gravy hop, high school hop, Hollywood hop, room service hop, routine hop, Sunday hop, true hop

• **difficult bounce to field**, caused by a rough infield
n. bad hop, cruel hop, in-between hop, nasty hop, tough hop, vicious hop, wicked hop

ground ball, hard-hit/sharp
n. ant-killer, brander, bug-bruiser, daisy clipper, daisy cutter, daisy dipper, daisy kisser, daisy scorcher, gopher hunter, grass cutter, grass trimmer, hot grounder/shot, lawnmower, scooter, scorcher, shin-skimmer, turfcutter, worm burner, worm killer

• hit a sharp ground ball
v. burn, clip, mow, scorch, shave, sizzle

• A hard ground ball may be "too hot to handle" for an infielder.

ground ball, weakly-hit
n. bleeder, bonk, cue-shot, dribbler, drizzler, knubber, nibbler, nubber, roller, squibber, swinging bunt, tapper, trickler, wriggler

• ground ball, weakly-hit, for a base hit
n. baby hit, Big Bill, dime hit, foozler, gorker, scratch hit

• hit a (weak) ground ball
v. bleed, cue, dink, dribble, nick, nub, pamper, roll, squib, tap, tick, tip, top

• Big Bill is thought to be named for third baseman Bill Bradley (1899-1915).

• If a fielder charges in for a weak ground ball and realizes that there is no play to be made at any base, particularly on the batter, the fielder holds on to the ball. This is known as "eating it" or "putting it in his hip (or back) pocket."

groundskeeper
n. groundhog (or ground hog), manicurist, sodfather; SPANISH preparador de terreno

• The head groundskeeper is in charge of the grounds crew (who may also be known as ground hogs).

• A wily grounds crew can have a sizable influence on a

ballgame. Above-average height for the infield grass can slow down a hot ground ball, allowing an easier play for an infielder. Wetting down the basepaths can slow down a speedy baserunner on the opposing team. When rain arrives, the grounds crew will rush to cover the field or take their sweet time depending on whether the home team is winning or not.

• The Philadelphia Phillies grounds crew in the middle of the 20th century were far less subtle. They constructed "Ashburn's Ridge," sloping the third-base line toward the field to keep the bunts dropped down by Hall of Fame center fielder Richie Ashburn (1948-1962) in fair territory.

H

Joe Connolly batting for the Washington Nationals in 1913 at an exhibition game at the University of Virginia, Charlottesville.
(Courtesy Library of Congress, LC-DIG-hec-02503.)

HBP (hit-by-pitch)
n. beaning, bruiser, hit batsman, plunking, strawberry raiser; SPANISH bateador golpeado

• hit a batter with a pitch
v. bean, bite, bruise, drill, nail, peg, plunk, soak, stick in the ear, strike, wing

• pitch that is meant to hit a batter, or come close to hitting a batter
n. beanball, bow tie, brushback, calling card, chin music,

duster, haircut, purpose pitch

• Beanballs and brushback pitches are, more often than not, ordered by the manager. The signal from a catcher for such a pitch is usually a fist with the thumb extended.

• A batter avoiding an inside pitch may bail out, dive, dodge, duck, hit the deck, hit the dirt, jackknife, limbo, skip rope, or tap dance.

• If a batter purposefully tilts or shifts his body so that the ball strikes him, it's said popularly that he "leaned into" the pitch and "took it for the team" (especially if the situation is helped out by a well-timed HBP).

"Some people give their bodies to science; I gave mine to baseball."

– second baseman Ron Hunt (1963-1974), hit by pitches 243 times in his career

hit (a pitched baseball)
v. birch, caress, carve, connect, cop off, deal, golf, knock, label, massage, meet the ball, plant, rattle, send, serve, strike, stroke; SPECIFIC fly, ground, line; SPANISH batear

• A batter "fashions a hit" when he hits safely.

• **hit a fly ball**
v. see *hit a fly ball* under *fly ball*

• **hit a ground ball**
v. see *hit a ground ball* under *ground ball*

• **hit a line drive**
v. see *hit a line drive* under *line drive*

hit with great force
v. air it out, bang, bash, baste, belt, biff, bing, blast, blaze, blow, bomb, boom, bop, buggywhip, bump, burn, bust, clip, clobber, clock, clout, club, cork, crank, crash, cream, crush, dent, drill, drive, get all of, go deep, hammer, hit a ton, jack, jar, jolt, juice, jump all over, jump on, kill, kiss, knock the cover off the ball, label, lace, ladle, lam, lambaste, laminate, land on, larrup, laser, lash, lather, launch, lay on, lay the wood on/to, lean against, lick, lit, mash, murder, nail, ozone, pack a punch, paste, pickle, pile into, plank, plaster, plug, poke, pole, pop, pound, pour the pine, powder, power, pummel, pulverize, put a charge into, put a jolt into, put the wood to, rake, ram, rap, rifle, rip, rock, rocket, sap, scald, scorch, sear, sizzle, slash, slam, slug, smack, smash, smite, smoke, soak, sock, spank, spike, square up, sting, stroke, swat, tag, tattoo, tear the cover off the ball, tee off, thump, thunder, torch, turn on, waft, wallop, whack, whale, wham, whang, whomp

• If a batter hits a ball hard (squarely, on the nose, on the screws, on the seams, or on the stitches) but is still put out, it is a "loud out."

• A batter's "wheelhouse" is where he can hit the ball best.

hit with barely any force
v. see *hit a (weak) ground ball* under *ground ball*

hit an inside pitch close to the hands ("get jammed")
v. fight off, fist, muscle

• A "jam-shot" is a ball hit by a batter when jammed.

• A "shank" is hit off the bat handle.

hit a pitch to the opposite field (when a right-hander hits the ball to right field or a left-hander hits the ball to left)
v. inside-out, jab, poke, punch, push, shoot, slice, spray

hit a pitch to the pull-field (when a right-hander hits the ball to left field, or a left-hander hits the ball to right)
v. drag, hook, jerk, pull, tug, turn on, yank

hit a pitcher with ease
v. batter, blast, blister, bomb, bombard, burn, clobber, destroy, drill, light up, manhandle, nail, own, paste, plaster, pound, pummel, rip, rock, rough up, shell, shellack, tattoo, tear into, thump, torch, wallop, wax, whip

• **begin hitting a pitcher with ease**
v. figure out, solve

• A number of hits in a row are considered bunched or clustered, forming a "barrage," "bombardment," "hitting bee," or "hit parade."

• If his offense was ripping through the opposition's pitching, scoring runs at will, broadcaster Red Barber would declare, "They're tearin' up the pea patch."

home plate
n. counting house, counting pan, counting station, dish, dock, hearth stone, home, home base, home turkey, marble, pan, pay station, pentagon, plate, platter, registry station,

rubber, saucepan, saucer, scoring iron, scratch, slab, turkey; SPANISH plato

• Home plate, pentagon-shaped and facing the catcher, is currently made of whitened rubber, though plates of the past were composed of iron, stone, or wood.

• Home plate is actually called "home base" in the official baseball rule book.

• The small broom used by the home plate umpire to clean off the plate is a brush or whisk. Baseball etiquette dictates that the umpires cleans the plate with his back to the field so that he never turns his rear end up at the fans behind the plate.

home run

n. Babe Ruth, Baker, Ballantine Blast, bell ringer, belt, big fly, big hit, big knock, big swat, biscuit, blast, bleacher reacher (or burner), bomb, bombski, bop, boundary belt, bullseye, bye-bye ball, circuit belt, circuit blow, circuit clout, circuit drive, circuit smash, circuit tripper, circuit wallop, connectamundo, cowhide joyride, day-tripper, dinger, ding-dong, drive, Dr. Long Ball, dong, downtowner, Federal Express, five dollar ride in a yellow cab, four-bagger, four-base hit, four-baser, four-cornered hit, four-cushion shot, four-master, four-ply blow, four-ply swat, four-ply wallop, four-sacker, four-timer, get-small-quick ball, goner, gopher ball, grand tour, hammer, home-bagger, homer, jack, long ball, long potato, long tater, looper, mammo bomb, master fly, missile, monster, monster shot, moon shot, poke, pop, potato, rainbow drop, rainmaker, rip, rocket, round-tripper, roundtrip ticket, roundtrip tour, scud, seat-boomer, shot, souvenir, spaceshot, stream of milk, swat, taco, tank, tape-measure job, tape-measure shot, tater, through trip, tonk, tour, upper fish, upper tank, up top, wallop, yak, yambo fly, yamma, yardball, yardwork, ya-ya; SPECIFIC grand slam, inside-the-park home run, leadoff home run, oppo (boppo), solo home run, three-run home run, two-run home run, walk-off home run; SPANISH cuadrangular, jonrón

• A home run that is hit without any teammates on base is a "solo shot" or a "monologue."

• A batter hitting a home run goes for a home run "trot," taking a "roundtrip tour" around the bases.

• A ball struck into the stands for a home run can be said to be "deposited" or "parked" there.

• Two consecutive home runs are hit "back-to-back." Three consecutive home runs are considered, without any sense of apparent irony or contradiction, "back-to-back-to-back."

• A "Baker" is named for Philadelphia Athletics Hall of Fame third baseman Frank "Home Run" Baker (1908-1922), who belted a pair of dramatic home runs in the 1911 World Series against the Giants and led the American League in homers from 1911 through 1914.

• A "Ballantine blast" was a home run for the New York Yankees in the years that Ballantine beer and ale sponsored the team's broadcasts.

• A batter hitting a home run is said to go "downtown," "long," or "yard."

• A home run hitter "dials long distance" (or dial either 8 or 9, the numbers used before dialing long distance in a hotel or at an office, respectively).

• An "oppo boppo" is a home run hit to the opposite field.

• A "stream of milk" was used to describe roundtrippers in both Ken Levine's *It's Gone! ... No, Wait a Minute...* (1993) and Robert Benson's *The Game* (2001), the latter referring to a Bob Costas home-run call.

• A "wall-scraper" barely makes it over the wall. This used to be pejoratively called a "Chinese home run."

• One of the most famous homers in World Series history occurred on October 15, 1988, Game 1 of the World Series between the underdog Los Angeles Dodgers and the powerful Oakland Athletics. With a full count and two outs in the bottom of the ninth, Dodgers pinch-hitter Kirk Gibson swatted a game-winning two-run homer off of Athletics untouchable closer Dennis Eckersley, lifting L.A. to a 5-4 victory. As it turned out, that plate appearance was the only one of the Series for the injury-plagued Gibson. The Dodgers went on to upset the A's in five games. The memorable radio and television calls of the dramatic home run:

"Gibson swings, and a fly ball to deep right field! This is gonna be a home run! Unbelievable! A home run for Gibson! And the Dodgers have won the game, 5 to 4! I don't believe what I just saw! I don't believe what I just saw!"

– Jack Buck, CBS Radio

"Sax waiting on deck but the game right now is at the plate. High fly ball into right field, she is gone! In a year that has been so improbable, the impossible has happened."

– Vin Scully, NBC-TV

• **easily-hit pitch, particularly for a home run**
n. avocado, barn door, batting practice fastball, beach ball, cantaloupe, cherry, cookie, cream puff, cupcake, fat one, fat pitch, gimme, gopher ball, grapefruit, groover, ham-and-cheese, hanger, hit-me pitch, lollipop, meatball, melon, mistake, pay ball, punkin, puss, room service pitch, salad, volleyball

"When you're hitting the ball, it comes at you looking like a grapefruit. When you're not, it looks like a black-eyed pea."

– first baseman George Scott (1966-1979)

I

First baseman Stuffy McInnis, second baseman Eddie Collins, shortstop Jack Barry, and third baseman Frank "Home Run" Baker were collectively nicknamed "The $100,000 Infield."
(Courtesy Library of Congress, LC-DIG-bbc-2046f.)

infield
n. carpet, diamond, inner garden, inner works; SPANISH cuadro adentro

• The "corners" of the infield are first and third base.

• A "fast" infield sees ground balls race into the outfield, barely affected down by the low-cut grass. A "slow" infield features higher grass, slowing down hard-hit ground balls so as to make defending them much easier for infielders.

• A smooth infield is a "pool table" and plays "true," without any bad bounces.

• An infield with more pebbles than grass is an "ash heap," "boneyard," "brickyard," or "rock pile." A "skin diamond" is an infield without any grass at all.

infielder

n. bagman, baseman, sacker, station keeper; SPECIFIC ancient mariner, corner infielder, Hoover, magician, matador, middle infielder, plumber, vacuum cleaner, Wilson Pickett, wizard; SPANISH fildeador de cuadro adentro

• Infielders may play "drawn in," "in," "halfway," "double-play depth," "back," or "deep."

• The first baseman and third baseman are the corner infielders. The second baseman and shortstop are the double-play combination or keystone combination (or "combo").

• The corner infielders may "pinch in" expecting a bunt, creeping closer to home plate.

• An infielder staying close to the first base or third base foul line is said to be "guarding" or "hugging" the line. When the corner infielders guard the lines late in the game, trying to prevent an extra-base hit, it is considered a "no-doubles defense."

• When the shortstop and/or the second baseman "cheat" toward second, they move closer to the bag before the pitch in anticipation of going for a force play and the possibility of turning a double play.

• An infield shift occurs when the infielders play out of their usual positions to better defend a hitter noted for hitting the ball primarily to one side of the diamond. When a defensive player moves slightly either to his right or left based on the batter and the situation, that player is said to be "shaded" in that direction.

• An excellent defensive infielder is "sure-handed" or has "soft hands."

• An "ancient mariner" is a poor defensive infielder who can be counted to only "stoppeth one of three," a quote from Samuel Taylor Coleridge's poem, "The Rime of the Ancient Mariner," and attributed to sportswriter Red Smith with regard to Hall of Famer Rabbit Maranville in the twilight of his career.

• A 'magician" or "wizard" is sensational defensively, with a tip of the cap to the "Wizard of Oz," Hall of Fame shortstop Ozzie Smith (1978-1996).

• A "matador" allows the ball to pass by with only the wave of his glove to show for any exertion of effort, a la the matador's "Olé!" and swipe of his cape as the bull charges past.

• A "plumber" is a skilled defender, stopping up any "leaks" that would allow a batted ball to find the outfield.

• A "vacuum cleaner" is a fielder who catches each ball hit to him with ease, as if he were using a vacuum to suck up the ball; such a player may also be called a "Hoover" after the specific brand of vacuum cleaner.

• A "Wilson Pickett" is a reliable infielder who uses a Wilson brand glove to "pick it" (field ground balls and line drives).

• An excellent defensive infield is a "stonewall."

• A poor defensive infield is a “sieve.”

• Connie Mack reportedly said of his talented Philadelphia Athletics infielders, “I wouldn’t take $100,000 for my infield.” From that point on, the quartet of first baseman Stuffy McInnis, second baseman Eddie Collins, shortstop Jack Barry, and third baseman Frank “Home Run” Baker were collectively nicknamed “The $100,000 Infield.” They lived up to their billing, winning the World Series in 1910, 1911, and 1913, and Collins and Baker ended up earning spots in the Baseball Hall of Fame alongside their proud manager.

inning
n. at-bat, canto, chapter, chucker, frame, heat, loop, period, round, session, spasm, stanza, verse; SPANISH entrada

• The visiting team’s at-bat is the top, top half, or upper half of the inning.

• The home team’s at-bat is the “bottom,” “bottom half,” “home half,” or “lower half.” “Last” may also be used, as in “The Blue Jays come to bat in the last of the seventh.”

• Up until 1950, the home team in the Major Leagues had the option of whether to bat first or last.

• The first, second, and third are the early innings, or the “early-going.”

• The fourth, fifth, and sixth are the middle innings.

• The seventh, eighth, and ninth are the late innings, or the “late-going.”

• A nine-inning game is "halfway to the house" in the middle of the fifth inning, halfway through the game.

• The seventh-inning stretch occurs in the middle of the seventh inning, featuring the singing of "Take Me Out to the Ballgame." If the game is extended to the fourteenth inning, a second stretch is usually added.

• The bottom of the ninth features the "last licks" (the last at-bat) for the home team.

K

Eddie Cicotte of the Chicago White Sox is credited by many for inventing the knuckleball. He's better known as a member of the 1919 Chicago Black Sox, banned from the game for throwing the World Series.
(Courtesy Library of Congress, LC-DIG-ggbain-13802.)

knuckleball
n. bob-and-weave, bubble, butterfly, bug, dancer, fingertip pitch, floater, flutterball, ghostball, knuckle, knuckler, moth, rabbit; SPANISH bola de nudillo, mariposa

"The trouble with throwing knuckleballs is that 95 out of 100 pitches have to be right. If you get only 85 out of 100, the 15 that miss are going to turn into eight triples, five doubles and a home run or two."

– Jim Bouton (1962-1970, 1978), *The Los Angeles Times*; June 2, 1971

• **pitch a knuckleball**
v. dance, float, flutter, knuckle, push, release

• "Knuckleball" is often a misnomer since a majority of knuckleballers throw the pitch off of their fingertips instead of their knuckles. The goal is to throw the baseball with as little spin as possible, causing the ball to move unpredictably through the air.

• "Mariposa" is Spanish for butterfly.

• Many of the names for the knuckleball depict its dancing, diving, floating, fluttering, swerving, tumbling, veering path toward the plate.

"I once asked umpire Augie Donatelli why he had called a knuckleball a strike. He gave me an answer I'll never forget. 'The pitcher doesn't know where it's going, the hitter can't hit it, the catcher can't catch it, and it's all over the ballpark before it gets here. It's been enough places that I figure sometime on the trip it must have crossed home plate for a strike.' "

- Joe Garagiola, *It's Anybody's Ballgame*

L

Babe Ruth and John McGraw before an exhibition game. Yes, the Babe is wearing a Giants uniform. *(Courtesy Library of Congress, LC-DIG-ggbain-36424.)*

league
n. circuit; SPANISH liga

• The National League (NL) is the senior circuit, dating back to 1876. The American League (AL) is the junior circuit, dating back to 1901.

• Until 1961 there were eight teams in each league. A team in the top four in its league was in the "first division." A team in the bottom four was in the "second division." In 1969, the leagues were each separated into Eastern and Western Divisions. The Central Division was introduced into each league in 1995, causing the current organization of teams. In 2013 the Houston Astros will shift to the American League, evening out the number of franchises in each circuit.

"I try to take a national view of the American League and an American view of the National League."
– Vice President Hubert H. Humphrey

• The "standings" list the won-lost record of each team in the league from best to worst, including winning percentage and "games back." For example, a team that has won two fewer games and lost two more games than another team is two games behind that team in the standings.

• The "magic number" shows how close a first place team is to clinching a league/division title or playoff berth, figured by adding one to the number of games remaining, subtracting the number of wins recorded by the leading team, and then subtracting the number of losses suffered by the trailing team. Every subsequent win by the leading team or loss by the trailing team subtracts one from the magic number. When the magic number reaches zero, the leading team clinches its league/division title or playoff berth.

• The "elimination number" is the opposite of a magic number, indicating how close a team is to being eliminated from postseason contention.

• Installed in the lexicon by broadcaster Red Barber, the first-place team in the league is said to be "in the catbird seat." A team or player in the catbird seat is one in a position of comfort and control. James Thurber later appropriated the phrase, as well as a number of other Barberisms, for his short story, "The Catbird Seat."

• The first-place team is also said to be "leading the way," "setting the pace," "sitting on top," and "looking down" on the rest of the league. Such a team may be positively categorized as a "dynamo," "powerhouse," "steamroller," and "the measuring stick" for the rest of the league.

• If a first-place team builds an extensive lead over its competition, that team is said to be "running away" with the division.

• A team that goes "wire-to-wire" is in first place all season.

• The last-place team is in the "basement," "cellar," or "dungeon." This team may be called the "cellar dweller," "cellar occupant," "cellar tenant," "doormat," "punching bag," or "tailender," "looking up" at the rest of the league.

"On a clear day they could see seventh place."
– Fresco Thompson, about the miserable 1920 Philadelphia Phillies

league pennant
n. flag, gonfalon, oriflamme, rag

• All of the above terms refer to the literal flag awarded to the team that won the American League or National League pennant and earned a berth in the World Series.

"These are the saddest of possible words:
"Tinker to Evers to Chance."
Trio of bear cubs, and fleeter than birds,
Tinker and Evers and Chance.
Ruthlessly pricking our gonfalon bubble,
Making a Giant hit into a double –
Words that are heavy with nothing but trouble:
"Tinker to Evers to Chance."

– "Baseball's Sad Lexicon,"
Franklin Pierce Adams, 1910

• Before divisions separated the American and National Leagues in 1969, a team in first place in its league at the end of the regular season captured the pennant. Now a team must battle through the regular season, the league divisional series, and the league championship series in order to win the pennant.

"There's a long drive.... It's gonna be, I believe... The Giants win the pennant! The Giants win the pennant! The Giants win the pennant! The Giants win the pennant!"
– Bobby Thomson's "Shot Heard 'Round the World"
Giants broadcaster Russ Hodges; October 3, 1951

left-handed pitcher
n. forkhander, hook arm, left-hander, lefty, loony Joe, off-side pitcher, portpaw, portsider, screw armer, southpaw, wrong armer; SPANISH zurdo

• The origin of the term "southpaw" is thought to be that baseball fields were designed with home plate facing east, making sure that the batter does not have to look into the sun. This put a left-handed pitcher's arm on the southside of the pitcher's mound.

• A right-hander ("righty" or "starboarder") may be jokingly called a "northpaw."

line drive
n. bee-liner, blue darter, bolt, bullet, clothesline, darter, firecracker, frozen rope, hemp, laser, liner, line shot, missile, rocket, screamer, screaming meemie, screaming rope, screecher, seed, shot, thunder bolt, ungodly shot, zinger; SPANISH linea

• hit a line drive
v. hang a clothesline, hang out a rope, hang out the clothes, hang out the wash, laser, line, rope

• A hard line drive is sharp, vicious, or wicked.

• A "humpback line drive" is a soft line drive, often easily fielded and rarely departing the infield.

• A line drive hit directly at a defensive player is called an "at 'em ball" or an "atom ball."

• Attributed to (and perhaps coined) by Red Sox second baseman Dustin Pedroia, a "laser show" features a slew of line drives bunched together, whether from the same player in subsequent at-bats or from a team's offense as a whole.

• The Double-A Southern League's Tennessee Smokies

play at Smokies Park, located at 3540 Line Drive in Kodak, Tennessee.

lineup
n. attack, nine, order, starting nine; SPANISH alineacion

• Each team's starting lineup is written down on a lineup card by the manager, with carbon copies presented at home plate to the opposing manager and the home plate umpire before the start of the game.

• Each spot (or slot) in the lineup may be referred to with its number. For example, the second batter is in the "2-hole."

• The top of the lineup is made up of "table-setters" and "igniters." The middle of the lineup is the "heart of the order" or the "meat of the order."

• A "balanced" lineup features a nonet of talented hitters. However, if there are any weak links, those poorer hitters are considered the "holes" in the lineup.

• The fourth-place batter is the "clean-up hitter."

• The ninth batter "rounds out the lineup" as the "second leadoff" batter.

• When all nine hitters come to the plate in the same inning, the team has "batted around."

• The lineup "flips" or "turns over" after the last hitter.

• It was 1929 when Babe Ruth first wore #3 and Lou Gehrig donned #4 to signify their spots in the batting order.

The rest of the lineup: Earle Combs was #1, Mark Koenig #2, Bob Meusel #5, Lazzeri #6, future manager Leo Durocher #7, and catchers Johnny Grabowski, Benny Bengough, and Bill Dickey wore uniforms 8 through 10. (Hall of Famer Dickey switched to #8 a year later.)

lose
v. acquiesce, cave in, cede, collapse, crash, crumble, droop, drop, fade, fall, falter, fizzle, flop, fold, give in, give up, go down, quit, slip, squander, stumble, submit, succumb, surrender, tap out, tumble, wave the white flag, yield; SPANISH perder

• **receive the defeat, as a pitcher**
v. eat, get, hit with, lose, pinned with, shoulder, suffer, swallow, take; SPANISH perder

"If you're a good loser, you keep on losing."
– manager Paul Richards (1951-1961, 1976)

losing streak
n. cold spell, drought, dry spell, schneid, slump, tailspin; SPANISH seguido perdiendo

• A team in the midst of a losing streak may be bombing, breaking down, choking, collapsing, crashing, cracking, crashing, cratering, crumbling, crumpling, deflating, degenerating, disintegrating, drooping, dropping, dying, fading, falling, falling apart, faltering, fizzling, flagging, flopping, floundering, folding, foundering, gagging, giving in, giving out, giving up, limping, lurching, out of whack, plummeting, reeling, sagging, scuffling, sinking, sliding, slipping, slumping, sputtering, staggering, stumbling, struggling, teetering, toppling, tottering, unraveling, waning, wilting, withering, or wobbling.

• No team got off to a worse start than the 1988 Baltimore Orioles, who lost their first 21 games of the season. The O's very first victory of the year waited until April 29. Baltimore finished the season with a 54-107 record, 34.5 games out of first place.

• The worst finish to a season belongs to the 1899 Cleveland Spiders, who managed to win only one of their final 41 games en route to a 20-134 record, 84 games out of first place. The Spiders were doomed purposefully by their ownership, which traded all of Cleveland's finest players to St. Louis – a team that they also ran. The neglected Spiders disbanded at season's end.

"Losing streaks are funny. If you lose at the beginning of the season, you got off to a bad start. If you lose in the middle of the season, you're in a slump. If you lose at the end, you're choking."

– attributed to manager Gene Mauch (1960-1982, 1985-1987)

loss

n. defeat, downfall, failure, fall, hiccup, L, slip, spill, stumble; SPANISH derrota, perdido

M

Clark Griffith and Connie Mack, still the record-holder among MLB managers for games managed and wins. *(Courtesy Library of Congress, LC-DIG-npcc-00309.)*

Major Leagues
n. big arena, big boys, big circus, big dance, big leagues, the bigs, big smoke, big time, big top, big yard, majors, MLB, the Show; SPANISH grande ligas

manager
n. big guy, boss, boss man, brains, captain, field general, field manager, general, head man, leader, maestro, the man, mastermind, old man, miracle man, pilot, professor, shepherd, skip, skipper, teacher; SPANISH diligente

• John "Mugsy" McGraw (1899, 1901-1932) was branded the "Little Napoleon." McGraw stood 5'7", an inch taller than Napoleon Bonaparte.

• "Gentleman George" Stallings (1897-1898, 1901, 1909, 1913-1920) was called the "Miracle Man" for bringing the 1914 Boston Braves (the "Miracle Braves") from last place in July to a National League pennant and a World Series title.

• The great Charles Dillon "Casey" Stengel (1934-1936, 1938-1943, 1949-1960, 1962-1965) was the "Ol' (or "Old") Perfessor."

• As described in Joe Garagiola's *It's Anybody's Ballgame,* a sign affixed in Whitey Herzog's office while he managed the Cardinals: " 'A slick way to outfigure a person is to get him figuring you figure he's figuring you're figuring he'll figure you aren't really figuring what you want him to figure you figure.' He wrote it himself."

"If you don't win, you're going to be fired. If you do win, you'll put off the day you're going to be fired."
– Hall of Fame manager Leo "the Lip" Durocher (1939-1946, 1948-1955, 1966-1973)

• remove a pitcher from the game
v. get, hook, lift, pull, remove, rescue, retrieve, save, send to the showers, stick a fork in him, take the ball away from, yank

• Hall of Famer George "Sparky" Anderson was known as "Captain Hook" while he managed the Cincinnati Reds (1970-1978) for his quick moves to the bullpen.

• The hit that causes the manager to remove a pitcher from the game is said to "chase" the pitcher, "knock" him out (of the box), or "send him to the showers."

• If the starting pitcher is removed from a game at the first sign of trouble, his manager likely has short patience and a "quick trigger."

"The best game managers, generally speaking, are those who have the courage to keep their hands in their pockets, let their players play and take the inevitable flak from the fans."

– Bill James, *Sport*, July 1984

Minor League player
n. bush, busher, farmhand, minor leaguer (or Minor Leaguer)

• See *baseball player, touted and young.*

• An "organizational" player is not believed to have Major League potential. Instead, a team signs him in order to fill out a Minor League roster and because he provides intangibles such as leadership and/or clubhouse chemistry as well as setting a positive example for higher-regarded but inexperienced (and perhaps immature as well) teammates.

• If a promising prospect has a player in the level directly above him who plays the same position (particularly if it is the Major Leagues), that prospect is considered to be facing a "road block."

• If a team has several minor leaguers who all play the same defensive position, that position is considered "deep"

– though it's very possible that there will be a "bottleneck" with the players either battling one another for regular playing time or facing road blocks in front of them. In such a situation, a position change or trade will likely be in order for one or several of the players, giving them a better opportunity to "contribute" or "break through."

• If a Major League team's front office personnel values a prospect, they'll make sure that he is placed in a position to enjoy the proper amount of playing time. In the case of a position player, such playing time is measured in terms of "at-bats." In the case of a pitcher, such playing time is measured in terms of "innings." For instance, a pitcher may well be sent down from the Majors back to the Minors if it is felt that he needs to receive more regular action in games (get more "innings under his belt").

• A "four-A" player is one who consistently excels at the Triple-A level but does not enjoy the same success in the Major Leagues.

• In *Ball Four*, published in 1970, Jim Bouton wrote, "Meal money in Triple-A is $7.50 a day. In the big leagues it's $15. I don't know if they mean to have you eat half as much or half as well." In 2011, minor leaguers received $25 per diem compared to $92.50 per diem for the men in the Majors. The larger amount may make a minor leaguer's eyes go wide, but in an article by Bob Sansevere of the *St. Paul Pioneer Press* on June 23, 2011, the majority of Minnesota Twins interviewed admitted that they gave most (if not all) of their per diem to clubhouse attendants.

Minor Leagues
n. bushes, bush leagues, the farm, minors; SPECIFIC affiliated ball, independent (or "indy") ball, lower levels,

unaffiliated ball, upper levels

• A Minor League team that is "affiliated" is linked to a Major League organization and is composed of players and staff designated by that Major League organization. An affiliated Minor League team is rarely owned by the Major League organization, though the Atlanta Braves own the majority of teams in their system and the St. Louis Cardinals own their Double-A affiliate in Springfield, Missouri.

• A "farm system" or "system" refers to all of the Minor League affiliates in a Major League team's organization.

• A farm system with a great deal of prospects ("brimming" or "overflowing with talent") is considered "deep," "fertile," "loaded," "rich," "stacked," or "stocked." A farm system without any prospects is "barren," "depleted," "drained," "empty," "lacking," or "poor."

• The Minor League network (or "ladder") comprising a farm system, from highest to lowest level:

1. AAA, or "Triple-A"
2. AA, or "Double-A"
3. A+, or "A-Advanced" (formerly known as "High-A")
4. A, or "Single-A" (formerly known as "Low-A")
5. Short-Season A, or "Short-A"
6. Rookie Ball

• There are two Triple-A Leagues: the Pacific Coast League and the International League.

• There are three Double-A Leagues: the Texas League, the Eastern League, and the Southern League.

• There are three A-Advanced Leagues: the Florida State League, the Carolina League, and the California League.

• There are two Single-A Leagues: the Midwest League and the South Atlantic League (also known as the "Sally League" for its SAL initials).

• There are two Short-A Leagues: the New York-Penn League and the Northwest League.

• There are four different American-based Rookie-level Leagues: the Appalachian League, the Pioneer League, the Arizona League, and the Gulf Coast League.

• Major League teams also have rookie-level teams in the Venezuelan Summer League and/or the Dominican Summer League.

• Every league from Triple-A through Single-A is considered a "full-season" league, playing from April till September. Short-A and Rookie-level are called "short-season" leagues, starting in June and playing half the schedule of the "full-season" leagues.

• Independent League teams are "unaffiliated," not connected to any Major League organization. Any MLB team that wishes to acquire a baseball player from the roster of an Independent League team must purchase that player's contract from that team's ownership. The 2013 Independent Leagues comprised the American Association, Atlantic League, Can-Am League, Frontier League, North American Baseball League, American West Baseball League, and Pecos League.

"This is kind of like purgatory. You're in between heaven

and hell, heaven being the big leagues and hell being anything other than baseball."
– former outfielder Von Hayes (1981-1992), while managing in the minors

move
v. advance, go, head toward, make one's way, proceed, progress, take, travel

move rapidly (running the bases or fielding)
v. barrel, book it, bolt, charge, chug, dart, dash, flash, flit, fly, gallop, gun, gun it, hasten, hightail, hoof it, hurry, lumber (if a larger player), motor, pelt, plug, press, push, race, roar, rumble, run, rush, scamper, scoot, scramble, scud, scurry, scuttle, shift gears, shoot, speed, sprint, stampede, storm, sweep, thunder, tear, vroom, whip, whisk, whiz, zip, zoom; SPANISH correr

• A player hustling for a base hit is said to "leg it out."

• An outfielder racing for a fly ball is "on the run" or "on his horse."

"If you get to one base and you can see the ball on the ground in the outfield, run like hell to the next base."
– shortstop Zoilo Versalles (1959-1971)

move slowly, due to injury
v. hitch, hobble, gimp, limp, stagger, stumble, totter

• A player's injury that slows him down (whether to his hamstring, ankle, foot, etc.) is described as a "bad wheel" or a "flat tire."

move slowly, with reluctance
v. dawdle, drag, drag (or move) a piano, pad, plod, schlep/shlep, shamble, shuffle, stomp, troop, trudge

• A player who does not give his best effort, particularly defensively, is said to "dog" it.

move without urgency
v. amble, boogie, breeze, cadillac, canter, coast, cruise, drift, gambol, glide, jog, loaf, lollygag, march, meander, mosey, nonchalant, parade, promenade, ramble, range, roam, sail, sashay, saunter, shimmy, slide, step, stride, stroll, strut, style, traipse, trot, waddle, walk, waltz, wander; SPANISH trotiando

• A batter "cadillacs" with an arrogantly slow home run trot.

Skip: "You lollygag the ball around the infield. You lollygag your way down to first. You lollygag in and out of the dugout. You know what that makes you?"
Larry: "Lollygaggers!"
Skip: "Lollygaggers."

– *Bull Durham* (1988)

N

Hippo Vaughn of the Chicago Cubs.
(Courtesy Library of Congress, LC-DIG-ggbain-16744.)

no-hitter
n. no-no; SPANISH juego sin hit

• A "no-hit bid" is a pitcher's attempt at a no-hitter.

• When a pitcher brings a no-hitter late into a game, he is said to be "flirting" with it.

• As Ken Levine writes in his 1991 Orioles broadcasting memoir *It's Gone! ... No, Wait a Minute...*, "There's always the question of just how an announcer should call a potential no-hitter. One school of thought is not to mention it at all (so as not to be a jinx), and the other says the broadcaster *must* discuss the situation. It is his responsibility to alert the audience to the potential historic feat. Chuck [Thompson], who has seen and called many a no-hitter, has a way of splitting the difference. He will say anything but the words 'no-hitter.' He will inform the listeners that the Orioles have yet to give up a hit, that the A's are hitless, that they're looking for their first base knock, etc., but he will not utter the phrase 'no-hitter.' "

• A pitcher with a no-hitter in progress, particularly if it is a perfect game, is ignored by his teammates when he sits on the bench. If anyone speaks with him, regardless of how much the pitcher might desire a good conversation, the no-hitter may be jinxed.

• An official scorer always hopes, as does everyone else attending, that the hit that breaks up a no-hit bid is a "clean" hit without any potential dispute as to whether it might have been an error.

• Hall of Famer Nolan Ryan (1966, 1968-1993) owns the record for most no-hitters, tossing seven of them in his career – in addition to 12 one-hitters (even with Bob Feller for the Major League record) and 18 two-hitters.

• There have been two recorded double no-hitters in professional baseball history. In a New York-Penn League game on August 20, 1952, Bradford's Frank Echtberger topped Batavia's Jim Mitchell, 1-0. More recently, in a Florida State League contest on August 23, 1992, Clearwater's Andy Carter shaded Winter Haven's Scott Bakkum, 1-0, thanks to a run on two walks and two sacrifice bunts in the seventh inning.

• On May 2, 1917, the Chicago Cubs' Hippo Vaughn and

Cincinnati Reds' Fred Toney matched hitless frames through nine innings before Cincy scratched out a run in the tenth against Vaughn for the victory. Toney completed the 10-inning no-hitter for a well-earned victory.

"Needless to say, I have more no-hitters than Nolan Ryan."
– Tigers broadcaster Ernie Harwell on his songwriting career
May 31, 2005, in the *Detroit Free Press*

O

Casey Stengel playing outfield for the Brooklyn Dodgers.
(Courtesy Library of Congress, LC-DIG-ppmsca-18466.)

offseason
n. hot stove league

• A "hot stover" is a baseball fan discussing the national pastime during the winter months.

"I'm looking forward to putting on my glasses with the fake nose so I can walk around and be a normal person."
– pitcher Dan Quisenberry (1979-1990), answering the question: "What do you plan to do after the [World] Series is over?"

opponent
n. adversary, antagonist, archrival, bad guy(s), bump in the road, challenger, competition, enemy, foe, nemesis, obstacle, opposer, opposite number, opposition, other side, rival, speed bump, spoilers, thorn; SPECIFIC cousin

• A player or team who plays with great success against an opponent is said to "own" them or "have their number."

• A "cousin" refers to a pitcher whom a batter hits easily, a batter who a pitcher dominates with ease, or a team that is easily and continually defeated.

• Usually a team only faces one opponent per game but on June 26, 1944, the New York Yankees, New York Giants, and the Brooklyn Dodgers all played one another at the Polo Grounds. The special exhibition was held to benefit the war effort, drawing over 50,000 in attendance. Six innings were completed, with each team facing its two opponents for two consecutive innings apiece. The victorious Dodgers scored five total runs against Yankee and Giant pitchers while the Yanks were held to one run and the Giants came up scoreless.

out
n. away, dead, done, down, finished, gone, off, retired, taken care of, turned away; SPANISH fuera

• There are three outs in a half-inning, six outs in an inning, and 27 outs for each team in a nine-inning game (though the home team does not use its last three outs if it is leading at the end of the top of the ninth, signaled by an "x" on the scoreboard and in the box score).

• When three outs are recorded in either team's at-bat, the side is retired.

• When three outs are recorded in the home team's at-bat, the inning is over.

• put out
v. cut down, deal with, dismiss, dispatch, dispose of, erase, finish off, get, kill, polish off, put away, retire, set down, take care of, vanquish

• three outs in a row in a half-inning, no runner reaching
n. go down quietly; one-two-three; set down in order; three up, three down

• A batter who is put out in each of his at-bats is said to "take an o-fer" or "wear the collar."

outfield
n. daisies, expanse, field, garden, lawn, meadow, orchard, outer garden, outer patch, outer works, outpost, pasture, suburbs; SPANISH bosque, cuadro afuera

• Right field is the "dexter meadow" or "right garden." Left field is the "left garden." Center field is the "middle pasture."

• The areas between left and center field ("left-center") as well as between center field and right field ("right-center") are the "alleys," "alleyways," "channels," "gaps," or "power alleys."

• A fly ball or line drive that drops between outfielders in either left-center or right-center is said to "drive," "flood," or "split" the gap. A more recent turn of phrase has the batter "shopping at the Gap."

• "Death Valley" refers to a deep outfield that turns potential extra-base hits into fly outs. Such an outfield may also be termed a "graveyard."

• "No man's land" is the area far beyond an outfielder's range where deep fly balls drop for extra-base hits.

• The "Bermuda Triangle" is the area where a shallow fly ball drops safely between three different defensive players, either two infielders and one outfielder or two outfielders and one infielder.

• A "sun garden" describes an outfield bathed in sunlight.

• In *Take Me Out to the Ballpark*, Josh Leventhal details the remarkable sight that was Clark Field, home of the University of Texas baseball team (and "various minor and negro league teams") from 1928 until 1974. "Fenway Park had the ten-foot "Duffy's Cliff" and Crosley Field had its outfield "terrace," but no ballpark, at any level of professional baseball, can compare to Clark Field at the

University of Texas for sheer oddity of terrain. The field had a full-blown bi-level outfield, with a 12-foot cliff separating the upper tier from the lower tier. This required outfielders to choose where they wanted to position themselves for a play: either stay on the lower field level and hope that the batter doesn't send the ball onto the upper outfield for a certain inside-the-park home run; or stand on the upper level and rely on the infielders and other outfielders to field line drives or short fly balls. It was just over 50 feet from the edge of the cliff to the wall in the deepest part of center. There was only one level in right field, as the outfield wall came right up to the cliff, but at only 300 feet from the plate, right field was nonetheless an inviting target for hitters."

outfielder
n. ball hawk, chaser, fly catcher, fly chaser, flyhawk, fly-retriever, gardener, grazer, hawk, orchardman, pastureman, pastureworker, picket, retriever, roamer, suburbanite; SPANISH fildeador de cuadro afuera, guardabosque

• The three outfielders together comprise the "picket line."

• The outfielders may play "deep," "shallow," "straightaway," "medium-depth," "toward the gaps," or "toward the lines."

• The left/right fielder are the "bookends" or the corner outfielders.

• The left fielder is on "left patrol" while the right fielder is on "right patrol."

• A "postage-stamp outfielder" is an outfielder with very little range, as opposed to the fine defensive skills of a "ball hawk" or a "fly-retriever."

• The "Million Dollar Outfield" (also known as the "Golden Outfield") referred to Boston's outstanding defensive trio of center fielder Tris Speaker, left fielder Duffy Lewis, and right fielder Harry Hooper, together from 1910-1915. Both Speaker and Hooper were later inducted into the Baseball Hall of Fame.

"Gee, it's lonesome in the outfield. It's hard to keep awake with nothing to do."
– Hall of Famer George Herman "Babe" Ruth (1914-1935)

outfield wall
n. barricade, barrier, boundary, divider, fence, garden wall, gate, padding, rampart; SPANISH pared, verja

• hit off the wall
v. bang, bounce, bound, careen, carom, clang, crack, crash, ding, glance, graze, hop, kiss, knock, pinball, pound, rap, rattle, rebound, ricochet, scrape, skim, smash, strike, thud, thump

• Harold "Pistol Pete" Reiser (1940-1942, 1946-1952) was already the best player in the National League at just 22 years old in 1941, finishing second in the Most Valuable Player Award voting to Brooklyn Dodger teammate Dolph Camilli. (Fellow teammate Whitlow Wyatt finished third in the voting.) But Pete Reiser's immensely promising career never reached its full potential, crushed by his own daredevil play and the hard outfield walls prevalent in ballparks at the time. Reiser's horrific collisions required 11 separate stretcher rides off the field, including one occasion that left him temporarily paralyzed and another that gave him a fractured skull.

• The walls in baseball are far more padded now than they were in Reiser's time, although there are exceptions. Golden Park in Columbus, Georgia, home to the South Atlantic League's Catfish from 2004-2008, features a solid brick outfield wall. The Chicago Cubs' storied home of Wrigley Field also has a brick wall, though it is covered by ivy. Alliant Energy Field in Clinton, Iowa, home to the Midwest League's LumberKings, has a wooden outfield wall, as does Birmingham's historic Rickwood Field, built in 1910, where the original concrete wall can still be seen behind the current wooden fence.

• The Metrodome, the Minnesota Twins' former home, featured a canvas wall in right field that covered up a section of seats used for football games. The wall was nicknamed the "Hefty Bag" – and jeered at by critics as a "trash bag."

"Winfield goes back, back.... He leaps.... His head hits the wall! It's rolling back toward second base! This is a terrible thing for the Padres."

– Jerry Coleman, voice of the San Diego Padres

P

Cy Young: The man, the legend.
(Courtesy Library of Congress, LC-DIG-ppmsca-18467.)

pennant
n. see *league pennant*

perfect game
n. masterpiece, perfect gem, perfection, perfecto; SPANISH juego perfecto

• A perfect game sees one team send 27 batters up and each set down in turn, with nary a baserunner to be seen. A base hit, a walk, a hit batsman, an error – anything that would cause a runner to reach "breaks up" a perfect game.

• The first perfect game in Major League history is credited to Worcester's Lee Richmond on June 12, 1880. Five days later, Hall of Famer John Montgomery "Monte" Ward twirled his own perfecto for Providence. Neither received much attention from the viewing public, though it would take 84 years before another National League pitcher was perfect (Philadelphia's Jim Bunning in 1964).

• On May 26, 1969, Pittsburgh left-hander Harvey "The Kitten" Haddix (1952-1965) spun 12 perfect innings against the powerful Milwaukee Braves, only to lose the game in the 13th inning on an error, an intentional walk, and a Joe Adcock home run. (The final score was just 1-0 due to runner Hank Aaron leaving the baseline rather than proceeding to the plate, rendering only the first run legitimate.)

• On June 2, 2010, Detroit right-hander Armando Galarraga set down the first 26 Cleveland Indians batters he faced. The 27th was rookie Jason Donald, who grounded to Tigers first baseman Miguel Cabrera. Cabrera tossed over to Galarraga covering first base, but umpire Jim Joyce ruled Donald safe. Replays revealed otherwise, but the perfect game bid had ended. Galarraga proceeded to retire the next batter, his "28th out," completing the Tigers victory. The well-respected Joyce apologized after the game. A postscript: the next day, Armando Galarraga was sent out to deliver the lineup card to that day's home-plate umpire, Jim Joyce. The two men embraced as the partisan Detroit crowd applauded.

"The million-to-one shot came in. Hell froze over. A month of Sundays hit the calendar. Don Larsen today pitched a no-hit, no-run, no-man-reach-first game in a World Series."

– Shirley Povich, *The Washington Post;* October, 1956

pitch

n. dealing, delivery, offering, serving, toss; SPECIFIC (as listed in *The Neyer/James Guide to Pitchers)* blooper, breaking ball, change-up, circle change, cut fastball, drop ball, drop curve, dry spitter, eephus, emery ball, fadeaway, fastball (or four-seam fastball), fingernail ball/fingertip ball, forkball, foshball, hard curve, incurve, inshoot, knuckleball, knuckle curve, outcurve, overhand curve, palm ball/wiggle ball, puff ball, raise ball, rising fastball, roundhouse curve, sailer, screwball, shine ball, short curve, sinker, sinking fastball, slider, slip pitch, slow ball, slow curve, slurve, sneak-ball, sneaky fastball, spike curve, spinner, spitball, split-fingered fastball, two-seam fastball, wiggle ball; SPANISH picheo; see *throw*
v. see *throw*; SPANISH pichar

"A pitcher needs two pitches, one they're looking for and one to cross them up."
– Hall of Fame pitcher Warren Spahn (1942, 1946-1965)

• See also "pitch a curveball" under "curveball"; "pitch a fastball" under "fastball"; "pitch a changeup" under "changeup"; "pitch a knuckleball" under "knuckleball"; or "pitch a slider" under "slider."

• Since the plate is 60 feet, six inches from the pitcher's mound, a pitch that bounces before it arrives is a "59-footer" (or a 58-footer, etc.).

Ways for a broadcaster to set up an incoming pitch:

1. The count: "The one-strike pitch," "The strike one pitch," "The 0-1," "Now the 0-1," "Here's the 0-1," "Here comes the 0-1," "The 0-1 delivery,"

"The 0-1 offering," "The 0-1 pitch," "The 0-1, on its way," etc.

2. Active action: "Lee brings it," "Lee deals," "Lee delivers," "Lee fires," "Lee hurls," "Lee pitches," "Lee serves it up," "Lee throws," "Lee twirls," etc.

3. Description: "Stieb cranks and fires," "Stieb kicks and throws," "Stieb rocks and delivers," "Stieb wheels and deals," "Stieb winds and serves it up," etc.

4. The classics: "The pitch," "Here's the pitch," "Here comes the pitch," "Pitch on the way," "The windup, and the pitch," etc.

"They've got a lot of names for pitches now, but there are only so many ways you can throw a baseball."
– Pete Reiser, while coaching the Chicago Cubs

pitch better in a tough situation (or "a jam")
v. battle, bear down, buckle down, grind, hump up, make a big pitch, man up, settle down, step up, stiffen, tighten up, toughen up

pitch effectively
v. breeze, coast, cruise, dazzle, deal, dictate, dominate, handle, mesmerize, mow down/through, mystify, own, paint, puzzle, reign supreme, roll, shove

• An effective pitcher is "dealing," "in rhythm," "in a groove," or "on his game."

pitch ineffectively
v. crack, falter, scuffle, stagger, struggle, stumble, throw batting practice (or BP), weaken, wobble

• An ineffective or rattled pitcher is considered to be "off his rhythm" or "off his game."

• A pitcher who is "laboring" is throwing a lot of pitches without results to show for it and may be visibly tiring on the mound. He may also be "losing his stuff."

pitch inside
v. back off, barber, brush back, bust inside, buzz, crowd, deck, deliver a message, dust, dust off, give a haircut, go headhunting, handcuff, jam, loosen up, put one in the kitchen, play sweet chin music, saw off, send a message, shackle, shave, tie up, trim

• Sal "The Barber" Maglie (1945, 1950-1958) received his nickname for his penchant for pitching so far inside, he regularly gave batters a "close shave." Maglie himself was perennially unshaven – and also was involved in two of the most famous games in baseball history. He was the starting pitcher for the New York Giants in the third game of their 1951 playoff series versus the Brooklyn Dodgers, which ended in Bobby Thomson's "Shot Heard 'Round the World." Switching allegiances to the Dodgers, he started Game 5 of the 1956 World Series and wound up on the wrong side of the first no-hitter in Major League postseason history, a perfect game tossed by the New York Yankees' Don Larsen.

pitch on the corners (the "edge" or "black" of the zone)
v. carve, chip, clip, cut, dab, glance, grab (the corner),

graze, kiss, nibble, nip, nudge, paint, scrape (the corner), shave, whisper, whittle

pitch with control
v. command, locate, master, paint, spot, spot up, stick, throw darts

• A pitcher with great control may also "waste" a pitch, purposefully throwing it outside the strike zone to tantalize, tease, or tempt the batter.

• The name given to a pitcher who finds himself suddenly unable to throw strikes is "Steve Blass disease." Blass (1964-1974) went 18-6 with a 2.12 ERA for Pittsburgh in 1968 and picked up a pair of victories in the 1971 World Series, won by the Pirates over the Baltimore Orioles. In 1973, the disorder struck, ending the hurler's career prematurely. "You have no idea how frustrating it is," said Blass in 1974. "You don't know where you're going to throw the ball. You're afraid you might hurt someone. You know you're embarrassing yourself, but you can't do anything about it. You're helpless. Totally afraid and helpless."

pitch, illegal
n. alternative pitch; POPULAR EUPHEMISM hard slider; SPECIFIC belt-buckle pitch, cut ball, dry spitter, emery ball, grease ball, jellyball, licorice ball, mud ball, paraffin ball, phonographic needle ball, pine tar ball, powder-puff ball, puff ball, quick pitch, quick return pitch, resin ball, sandpaper ball, scuffball, scuffed ball, scuffer, shine ball, shiner, spitball, talcum ball, Vaseline ball

• See "spitball" for the most well-known of all illegal

pitches.

• From *Baseball Anecdotes* by Daniel Okrent and Steve Wulf: "[Hall of Fame pitcher Don] Sutton was often accused of doctoring baseballs to his liking. Asked if it was true he used a 'foreign substance,' Sutton said, 'Not true at all. Vaseline is manufactured right here in the United States of America.'"

"If you can cheat, I wouldn't wait one pitch longer."
– manager George Bamberger (1978-1980, 1982-1983, 1985-1986), advising a struggling pitcher

pitcher
n. arm, artillerist, ball tosser, battery mate/batterymate, box artist, boxman, chucker, elbow bender, fifth infielder, flinger, flipper, giver, hand grenader, heaver, hillman, hurler, hurlester, hurlsmith, hurlster, man on the firing line, man on the mound, mound artist, moundsman, pill slinger, slab artist, slabber, slabbist, slabman, soupboner, souper, tosser, twirler, worker; SPANISH lanzador

• **pitcher, ace starting**
n. #1 starter, ace, anchor, bell cow, bellwether, meal ticket, Michelangelo, Picasso, stopper

• **pitcher, durable**
n. horse, innings eater, innings guy, innings monster, workhorse

• **allow (hits or runs)**
v. cough up, (get) reached for, give up, serve up, surrender, yield

• A team's group of pitchers is called its "pitching corps," "stable," or the team's "arms." Likewise, a "stablemate" is one's fellow pitcher on the team.

• A team's starting pitchers are known as the mound corps, staff, or starting rotation. Teams generally utilize a four-pitcher or five-pitcher rotation, though the four-man rotation has gone largely out of vogue.

• The #1 and #2 starters on a team are the top or front end of the rotation. The #2, #3, and #4 starters are the middle of the rotation. The #4 and #5 starters are the back end of the rotation.

• A pitcher's arm slot is the angle at which he releases the ball. A pitcher may throw overhand ("right over the top" or "from his ear"), three-quarter angle, sidearm, or submarine.

• With the bases empty, a pitcher usually works out of the full windup (or "windmill"). With a runner on base, a pitcher usually works out of the stretch or slidestep in order to prevent a potential steal.

• The pitches that a pitcher throws are his arsenal, bag of tricks, repertoire, or stuff. If a pitcher is doing well, that pitcher's stuff is "working." If a pitcher is highly talented, his stuff may also be considered dirty, disgusting, filthy, lights-out, nasty, or wicked – all spoken in very complimentary fashion.

• A pitcher "keeps the hitter honest" (or off-balance) by "mixing it up" with an assortment of different pitches.

• A well-pitched game is a gem, jewel, or masterpiece.

• A pitcher who throws a complete game "goes the distance" and "finishes what he started."

• A pitcher's best pitch is his ace, bread-and-butter, cash cow, Sunday best, or Sunday pitch.

• A pitcher who pitches "backward" throws his off-speed and breaking pitches early in the count and his fastball late. It's considered backward since a pitcher's first pitch is a fastball the majority of the time.

• A pitcher who throws temptingly high pitches, trying to get the batter to chase them outside of the strike zone, is "climbing the ladder," "stair-stepping," or "stair-stuffing."

• A "bulldog" or "grinder" battles each hitter with grit rather than finesse or style.

• A pitcher with a "rubber" arm is able to throw a great deal of pitches, not tiring easily.

• A "Houdini" is a pitcher who manages to consistently escape unscathed from jams potential offensive rallies, without any major damage done. The most threatening jam a pitcher faces is a bases-loaded, none-out situation; an escape without any runs scoring is a true "Houdini act," named for magician and escape artist Harry Houdini (1874-1926).

• A fine defensive pitcher is a "cat."

• A "feel" pitcher may not have dominating stuff, but "knows how to pitch," succeeding thanks to his wits, wiles, and mound acumen.

• When a pitcher "crosses up" the batter or the catcher, he throws a pitch that wasn't expected. It's the best strategy for dealing with the batter, but it's potentially disastrous for the surprised catcher.

• A pitcher who supplies a key base hit is said to "help his own cause."

"I always felt the pitcher had the advantage. It's like serving in tennis."

– Allie Reynolds

pitcher's mound
n. bump, crest, firing line, hill, hillock, hilltop, incline, knoll, mound, mountain, summit; SPANISH lomita

• meeting on the pitcher's mound
n. assembly, colloquium, chat, con-fab (a classic Ernie Harwellism), conference, congress, conversation, convocation, council, dialogue, discussion, exchange of ideas, fiesta, forum, huddle, meeting of the minds, party, powwow, rally, round table, seminar, symposium, talk, tea party

• take the mound in order to pitch
v. ascend, climb, mount, scale, walk up

• Once the pitcher stands atop the mound, he gazes, glares, glowers, leans in, looks, peers, squints, or stares in for the sign.

• A ball "combed" is hit directly back toward the mound, termed a comebacker, boomerang ball, or pearod. If it gets past the pitcher, the ball is said to go through the "originator," through the box, or through the pitcher's box.

pitcher's rubber

n. slab; SPANISH goma de pichar

• A pitcher may be described as "toeing" or standing on the rubber either in the middle, on the first-base side, or on the third-base side.

• A pitcher standing on the mound but not touching the rubber is said to "straddle" it.

pop fly
n. pop, popper, pop-up; SPECIFIC home run in a bandbox, home run in an elevator shaft, home run in a silo, Little League pop-up, Major League pop-up; SPANISH bombo, fly alto

• hit a pop fly
v. see *hit a fly ball*" under *fly ball*

• A pop fly above home plate is also said to travel "up the chimney," "up the chute," "up the elevator shaft," "up the shaft," or "up the silo."

R

Cheers for Heinie Zimmerman of the New York Giants.
(Courtesy Library of Congress, LC-DIG-ggbain-25474.)

record
n. achievement, accomplishment, benchmark, high, mark, milestone, standard, standard of excellence

• break a record
v. beat, best, better, cap, clear, eclipse, exceed, overstep, overtake, pass, shatter, snap, surmount, surpass, top, trump

• set a record
v. carve out, compile, create, erect, establish, forge, put together, write one's name in the record books

"Fifty years from now I'll be just three inches of type in a record book."

– Hall of Fame third baseman Brooks Robinson (1955-1977), *Sport*; October 1963

relief pitcher
n. bullpenner, reliever; SPECIFIC caddy, closer, early-long man, ham-and-egg reliever, LOOGY, long man, middle reliever, middle-long man, middle-short man, mop-up man, secondary closer, set-up man, short man, situational lefty, vulture; SPANISH apagafuego, pelevista

• A bullpen generally is composed of mop-up men (when the game's outcome is not in doubt), middle relievers (for the middle innings), set-up men ("caddies," used in the late innings), and the closer (to save the game).

• Relievers are also divided into "long relievers" or "long men," who can work multiple innings effectively, and "short relievers" or "short men," whose effectiveness dims the longer they remain in the game.

• When the first relief pitcher enters the game, he's the first "out of the chute."

• A "ham-and-egg" reliever is consistent but unspectacular.

• A "LOOGY" ("lefty one-out guy") is a "situational" left-handed pitcher who is brought into the game to face one left-handed batter and is removed immediately following that at-bat no matter the result.

• A "vulture" is a relief pitcher who enters a game with the lead, gives it up, and then picks up the victory when his offense retakes the lead for good.

• A bullpen "stirring" sees a reliever (or relievers) standing up and stretching before starting to "loosen" or warm up.

• "Action" in the bullpen occurs whenever a relief pitcher begins to warm up. Such a bullpen would also be considered "busy" or "at work."

• "Double barrel action" occurs when a right-handed and left-handed pitcher warm up at the same time in the bullpen.

• The first batter to face a relief pitcher is said to "greet" or "welcome" that reliever to the mound.

"Why pitch nine innings when you can get just as famous pitching two?"

– pitcher Albert "Sparky" Lyle (1967-1982)

run

n. ace, counter, mark, marker, notch, picket, score, tally; SPANISH carrera
v. see *move with urgency*

• Note that for all of the different terms used to mean a "run" in baseball, the word "point" (favored in basketball, football, and tennis) is never used.

• 0, on the scoreboard
n. bagel, blank, blank spot, donut, egg, Firestone, goose egg, hen fruit, nada, nothing, zero, zip, zippo; SPANISH zero

• 1, on the scoreboard
n. matchstick, singleton, solo tally; SPANISH uno

• 8, on the scoreboard
n. snowman; SPANISH ocho

• Aside from 0, 1, and 8, no other numbers have been accorded nicknames.

• A "blind," "blinder," or "clean frame" is a scoreless inning.

• A scoreless game in Spanish is *sin anotaciones*, meaning without runs.

• Any number of runs larger than 1 is a "crooked number," which a team "puts up" or "hangs" on the scoreboard during a big inning.

• A game with a lot of runs may "light up the scoreboard like the Fourth of July."

• Runs added to a narrow lead late in the game are called "insurance runs."

• A run that locks up a victory "salts away the win," "puts icing on the cake," "sticks a fork" in the opponent, and (in the words of Red Barber) "ties up the crocus sack."

run batted in (RBI)
n. rib, ribbie, ribbee, ribeye, steak; SPANISH carrera empujada

• bat in a teammate
v. bring home, bring in, come through, deliver, drive home, drive in, knock home, knock in, plate, produce, score, send plateward

rundown
n. hotbox, pickle

• A baserunner in a rundown is "hung up" or "in the jug."

• The most famous failed rundown in baseball history occurred on October 15, 1917, forever nicknamed thereafter as "Heinie's Mad Dash." It was Game 6 of the World Series, pitting the powerful Chicago White Sox (who would throw the series only two years later) against the dynastic New York Giants. The White Sox needed one more win to clinch the championship. In the top of the fourth inning, Chicago placed runners at first and third. Happy Felsch grounded back to Giants pitcher Rube Benton, and runner Eddie Collins found himself trapped off third base. The ball ended up in the hands of third baseman Heinie Zimmerman, who chased Collins toward home – but there were no Giants covering the plate. The White Sox went on to win the game, and the World Series, 4-2. The sight of "The Great Zim" waving the ball in his hand and running hopelessly behind the fleet Collins in an unwinnable race to the plate was oft-imitated during the off-season, particularly by Collins himself.

S

A player sliding into home.
(Courtesy Library of Congress, LC-USZ62-135410.)

save

v. clinch, lock up, nail down, preserve, seal the deal, shut the door, slam the door, stave off; SPANISH salvar

• The save statistic was invented by Chicago sportswriter and historian Jerome Holtzman and was adopted by Major League Baseball in 1969. One of the more controversial stats with regard to its effectiveness, a pitcher receives a save for 1) pitching the final three innings of his team's victory; 1) pitching the final inning of a victory and protecting no more than a three-run lead; or 3) entering the game with the potential tying run in the on-deck circle and recording the final out(s) of a victory. A pitcher should not be credited with both a win and a save in the same game.

schedule
n. agenda, calendar, card, docket, guide, log, map, sked, slate; SPANISH calendario

score
n. count; SPANISH anotacion
v. chalk up, compile, notch, plate, pile on, pile up, post, put up (on the scoreboard), rack up, tally

• tie the score
v. balance the budget, deadlock, equalize, even, knot, match, pull even, square

• take (the lead/advantage)
v. gain, grab, jump ahead, jump in front, pass, seize, snatch, surpass

• lose (the lead/advantage)
v. blow, cough up, give up, relinquish, surrender, yield

• The team in the lead may also be stated to "have the advantage," be "out in front," or be "ahead" of its opponent.

• A team that provides a lead for its pitcher is said to "stake" the pitcher to that lead.

• The team that is not in the lead is behind, down, facing a deficit, looking up, or trailing.

• A particularly large deficit is regarded as a "mountain to climb."

scout
n. bush shaker, bushwhacker, ivory hunter, talent evaluator; SPECIFIC advance scout, area scout, area supervisor, bird dog, checker, cradle-snatcher, crosschecker (national or regional), eye-in-the-sky (or spy in the sky), regional scout, scouting consultant, scouting coordinator, scouting director, snowbird, special assignment scout, superscout

• As George Will writes in *Men at Work*, "[An advance scout's] subject is the upcoming opponent's tendencies. Advance scouts are paid to be tendency-prone. Such a scout is a sort of spy, but he is quite open about it. In fact, there is a nice camaraderie among such intelligence agents as they sit behind the screen behind home plate in ever Major League park. They are armed with stopwatches to time pitchers' and catchers' release times… and batters' times running to first base. They also have charts and, sometimes, radar guns to time the velocity of pitches."

• A "bird dog" refers to an associate scout, or to a scout's friend or contact.

• A "snowbird" is a northern scout who goes south for the baseball season.

"When I was 21, I could throw a baseball 92 miles an hour. This led to a strange courtship between my left arm and a series of pencil-mustached, overweight, middle-aged men."
– Minor League pitcher Matt McCarthy; the first two sentences of his memoir, *Odd Man Out*

screen (behind home plate and often the dugouts, protecting fans from dangerous foul balls)
n. divider, life-saver, mesh, net, netting, partition, web, webbing, wiring; SPANISH protectora

• The word "protective" may be added to the front of any of the above terms.

screwball
n. butterfly curve, corkscrew, incurve, reverse curve, screwgie, scroogie; SPANISH bola tornillo

• New York Giants Hall of Famer Christy Mathewson (1900-1916) used the "fadeaway," his own version of the screwball.

• A different Giants great, Hall of Fame left-hander "King" Carl Hubbell (1928-1943) also used the screwball to terrific results. Hubbell attended Tigers spring training, but Ty Cobb was convinced that the young pitcher was going to injure himself by throwing the screwball, banned him from using it, and later released him. Since the Giants had succeeded with Mathewson's screwball usage, the New York squad took a chance on Hubbell in 1928 and never regretted the decision. Six years later, at the 1934 All-Star Game, "The Meal Ticket" struck out five consecutive American League legends – Babe Ruth, Lou Gehrig, Jimmie Foxx, Al Simmons, and Joe Cronin – and cemented his name in baseball lore.

season
n. campaign, term, year; SPANISH temporada

• Two of the most popular sayings, whether wise or clichéd, with regard to the season:
"It's a marathon, not a sprint."
"I'm taking it one game at a time."

second base
n. keystone, middle station, midway, midway station, second, second station; SPANISH segunda base

series
n. set, tilt; SPANISH serie

• The first game in the series is the opener.

• The last game in the series is the finale.

• A decisive series finale is the "rubber match."

• When one team wins more games than another in a series, that team "wins" the series. When two teams win the same number of games in a series, they "split."

• If one team wins every game in a series, that team is said to "take out the brooms" and "sweep" the series. As Peter Morris observes in *A Game of Inches,* "The use of brooms to commemorate a sweeping victory or a series sweep is much older than today's fans might expect. It appears that brooms were initially used by visiting spectators in hopes that their association with witchcraft would bring bad luck to the home team. Their popularity was probably also aided by the fact that they helped identify a small group of spectators who were rooting for the visiting team."

sidearmer

n. sidedealer, sidewheeler, sidewinder, subway slinger; SPANISH tira por el lado del brazo

• When a pitcher throws from the sidearm angle, he "drops down."

• A pitcher who throws the ball from an exaggeratedly low angle is a "submariner." He is also facetiously called an "Australian," since he throws the ball from "Down Under."

"There's a ballplayer who does two things at the same time. He pitches – and digs for oil."

– Cookie Rojas (1962-1977) on submariner Ted Abernathy, *Baseball Digest;* August, 1968

single

n. bagger, base hit, bingle, bingo, infield hit (if the ball does not reach the outfield grass), knock, one-bagger, one-base hit, one-sacker, safety, seeing-eye single (if the ball barely avoids a fielder or a couple of fielders, also called a "ball with eyes on it"), solitaire; SPANISH sencillo

• "Small ball" or "little ball" occurs when a team uses singles, sacrifices, stolen bases, and well-occasioned groundouts to "scratch out" runs, rather than scoring via an offensive barrage of extra-base hits.

• As the Major League's all-time career hits leader with 4,256, it makes sense that Pete Rose (1963-1986) would own the career record for singles as well. He does, with 3,215. Rose never notched over 200 singles in a season, however, a distinction that belongs solely to "Wee" Willie Keeler (206 singles in 1898) and Ichiro Suzuki (225 singles in 2004; 203 singles in 2007).

"Hit 'em where they ain't."
– hitting philosophy of Hall of Famer Willie Keeler (1892-1910)

sinker/sinkerball
n. drop, dropper, dropball (or drop ball), heavy ball; SPECIFIC sinking fastball; SPANISH bola que se unde

• pitch a sinkerball
v. bury, dip, drop, sink

• A sinker is said to "disappear," "fall off the table," or "have the bottom fall out."

• A pitcher who throws sinkers, or a "sinkerballer," is noted for being a "ground-ball pitcher."

slide
n. SPECIFIC backdoor slide, belly slide, belly whopper, bent-leg slide, break-up slide, Chicago slide, fadeaway, fallaway slide, half gainer, headfirst slide, hook slide, pop-up slide, scissors slide, stand-up slide, straddle slide, take-out slide; SPANISH tirada, deslisaje
v. bite the dust, dive, get dirty, get down, go in low, hit the dirt; SPANISH deslisarse

• Hall of Famer Mike "King" Kelly (1878-1893) was a figure of tremendous renown in pro baseball's early days, known for his flamboyance off the field, performing in theater and vaudeville in the off-season, as well as for his flashiness on the field. An electrifying baserunner, Kelly gained particular notice for his "hook slide," throwing himself forward feet first and reaching out with his hand to swipe safely at a base or home plate. In 1889, the wildly popular song "Slide, Kelly, Slide" was released. In 1927, MGM put out a comic film with the same title.

"It was while traveling to Boston for Mike Murphy's Burlesque Corps in the fall of 1894 that Kelly caught a cold that turned to pneumonia. He was taken to the hospital on a stretcher on November 5, and while some claimed he fell off the stretcher, and others said he was dropped while going up the stairs, there was no dispute as to his final words. 'This is my last slide,' he whispered; three days later he was gone."

– Daniel Okrent & Steve Wulf, *Baseball Anecdotes*
("This is me last slide" is another version of Kelly's words.)

slider
n. biter, dinky curve, nickel change, nickel curve, sailer, slide ball, slide beat, slide piece, snapper; SPECIFIC back door slider, back foot slider, back-up slider, hard slider, power slider, sweeping slider; SPANISH bola que se delisa

• pitch a slider
v. backdoor, break, hook, slice, slide, snapdragon, snap off, sweep, twist

• A slider is a cousin of the curveball but is thrown harder with more sideways (rather than downward) movement. Either George Blaeholder (1925, 1927-1936) or George Uhle (1919-1934, 1936) is regularly named as the originator of the slider.

• A "back-foot slider" breaks at the back foot of the batter.

• A "back-door slider" starts off outside, then veers back

across the outside corner (thereby entering into the strike zone via the "back door"). The opposite is a "back-up slider" which cuts back across the inside corner, often by accident.

• A "slurve" is a hybrid slider-curveball.

slump
n. cold spell, drought, dry spell, rough spot, schneid, skid, slide, struggle; SPANISH mal rato

spitball (illegal)
n. aqueous toss, bola ensalivada, brown spitter, bubble-gum ball, country sinker, Cuban forkball/palmball, cuspidor ball, cuspidor curve, damp sling, drooler, drop ball, eel ball, expectoration pellet, geyser ball, humidity dispenser, moist ball, moist curve, moisture ball, perspiration pellet, pump pellet, rain rippler, saliva heave, saliva toss, saliva twist, saturated curve, slick sling, slobber ball, soggy delivery, spitter, Staten Island sinker, super-sinker, sweat ball, vapor float, wet ball, wet delivery, wet one, wet pitch, wet wipe

• A pitcher preparing a spitball "loads up the ball."

• The last pitcher allowed to throw the spitball, grandfathered in after the pitch was outlawed, was "Ol' Stubblebeard" Burleigh Grimes (1916-1934). Grimes named his spitter the "drugstore drop."

"Cheating is baseball's oldest profession. No other game is so rich in skullduggery, so suited to it or so proud of it."
– sportswriter Thomas Boswell, *Inside Sports*, 1981

sportswriter
n. correspondent, journalist, media, member of the press, press, reporter, scribe, scrivener, writer; SPECIFIC cub, beat writer, blogger, chipmunk, columnist, commentator, contributor, hack, media person, newspaperman, newspaper writer, penner, stringer, television reporter; SPANISH cronista deportivo

• A generation of young New York sportswriters in the 1960s were termed "chipmunks" since they went "digging for nuts" in the clubhouse, searching for information for articles and columns.

"You have to watch out for those reporters. They ask you questions, they write down your answers, and then they put 'em in the paper."

– pitcher Bill Fischer (1956-1964)

stadium
n. see *baseball field*

starting pitcher
n. starter; SPANISH abridor

Ways to describe the next day's starting pitcher:

1. To the point: "Mathewson will start," "Mathewson to start tomorrow," "Mathewson will be the starter."

2. Team's (or manager's) choice: "The Braves will go with Glavine." "The Braves tab Glavine as the starter," "The Braves send Glavine to the mound," "Glavine receives the start for the Braves,"

"Glavine gets the ball for the Braves."

3. Using the pitcher's mound: "Santana will be on the bump," "Santana will take the hill," "Santana will take the mound," "Santana will toe the rubber."

"You hear ten people ask, 'Who is going to pitch for the Yankees tomorrow?' where you don't hear one ask, 'Who is going to be elected?' "

– humorist Will Rogers; September 24, 1928

stolen base
n. burglary, heist, SB, steal, swipe, theft; SPECIFIC delayed steal, double steal, straight steal, triple steal; SPANISH base robada

• **take a lead off/from (a base)**
v. dance off, ease off, measure out, sidle out, step from, step off, stretch out, take kangaroo hops, walk off, wander off

• **steal (a base)**
v. abscond, appropriate, bag, burglarize, capture, carry off, carry the mail, cop, embezzle, fiddle, filch, grab, lift, make off with, nab, pilfer, pinch, poach, purloin, rip off, snatch, swipe, take, thieve; SPANISH robar

• A successful stolen base is "executed" or "pulled off."

• A "straight steal" sees a runner take off on a stolen base attempt as the pitcher goes into his motion. A "delayed steal" sees the runner hesitate until the pitch has already been thrown and the defense has ceased to pay attention to him before taking off.

• A successful double steal sees two runners steal a base on the same play.

• The exceedingly rare triple steal sees a bases-loaded situation where all three runners somehow manage to move up a base, including a daring steal of home plate by the runner from third base.

• The Major League leader in stolen bases is Hall of Famer Rickey Henderson (1979-2003), who nabbed 1,406 steals over the course of his career. Henderson peaked with 130 stolen bases in 1982, the most in the modern era.

• Scottish-born Hugh Nichol (1881-1890) is given credit for 138 stolen bases in just 125 games for the American Association's Cincinnati Red Stockings in 1887. It wasn't a fluke, either. In 1882, Nichol swiped 103 more bases.

"Lou Brock was the symbol of great base stealing. But today, I'm the greatest of all time."

– Rickey Henderson upon breaking Brock's career stolen base record; May 1, 1991

strikeout

n. bat the breeze, Casey act, dipsy-doodle, fan, fandango, gate, K, line drive to the catcher, Navy Yard home run, punch-out/punchout, three strikes, whiff; SPANISH ponche

• A large number of strikeouts in a row form a "fanning bee."

• A pitcher's "out" pitch is the pitch he throws in order to record a strikeout, "finishing off" the batter.

• If a pitcher faces the minimum of three batters in a half-inning and strikes each one out with exactly three pitches, he's achieved the rare feat of an "immaculate inning."

• Nolan Ryan owns the Major League pitching record with 5,714 strikeouts notched in his career, 839 more than Randy Johnson's second-most total. Ryan also owns the modern record for most strikeouts in a single season, whiffing 383 batters in 1973.

• On September 12, 1962, Washington Senators right-hander Tom Cheney (1957, 1959-1964, 1966) battled his way to 21 strikeouts in a 2-1, 16-inning victory over the Baltimore Orioles, setting a record for most whiffs by one pitcher in a game.

• The pitching record for most strikeouts in nine innings is 20, accomplished twice by Roger Clemens on April 29, 1986, and September 18, 1996; once by 20-year-old Kerry Wood on May 6, 1998; and once by Randy Johnson on May 8, 2001 (though the game proceeded into extra innings).

"Baseball is almost the only orderly thing in a very unorderly world. If you get three strikes, even the best lawyer in the world can't get you off."

– Bill Veeck

strike out swinging, as a batter (scored as a normal "K") *v.* come up empty, fan, get buried, get rung up, go down fishing, K, ozone, pull a Casey, take a drink, whiff

• "Pulling a Casey" refers to the mighty slugging titular hero of Ernest Lawrence Thayer's poem, "Casey at the Bat," who is struck out swinging to end the ballgame.

strike out looking, as a batter (scored as a reverse "K")
v. admire a third strike, catch looking/napping, freeze, go down standing/looking/watching, watch strike three, take strike three (or a "called" strike three)

"He was out for excessive window-shopping."
"He stood there like the house by the side of the road."
– classic Ernie Harwell-isms

• Broadcaster Ernie Harwell's classic phrase "stood there like the house by the side of the road," affixed upon an opposing batter who struck out looking, was an allusion to the poem "The House by the Side of the Road" by Sam Walter Foss (1858-1911). The final two verses of the poem: "Let me live in my house by the side of the road /And be a friend to man."

• A batter who is 0-for-4 with four strikeouts wears the "golden sombrero."

• A batter who is 0-for-5 with five strikeouts wears the "platinum sombrero" (or visor) or "Olympic Rings."

strike zone
n. plate, zone

• In the early days of baseball, the strike zone stretched from the batter's shoulders to his knees. According to the Major League Baseball Official Rule Book, the current strike zone is the "area over home plate the upper limit of which is a horizontal line at the midpoint between the top of the shoulders and the top of the uniform pants, and the lower level is a line at the hollow beneath the kneecap. The Strike Zone shall be determined from the batter's stance as the batter is prepared to swing at a pitched ball."

Ways to describe a pitch's location in the strike zone:

1. Using the batter's body: at, above, or below the spikes, shins, knees, waist, belt, belly, letters (on the front of the uniform), shirt, chest, hands, or shoulders. The pitch can also be thigh-high, knee-high, waist-high, belt-high, belly-high, letter-high (or letters-high), chest-high, or shoulder-high.

2. Using the batter's zone: "in there" (any pitch in the strike zone), inside, outside, low, high, inside corner, outside corner, inside edge, outside edge, inner half, outer half, top half, bottom half, upper half, lower half.

3. Middle of the strike zone: down Broadway, down Main Street, down the alley, down the pike, down the pipe, grooved, heart of the strike zone, served up, split/cut the plate in half.

4. Inside: close, in, in the kitchen, near, (too) tight.

5. Outside: away, a ways away, far, wide.

6. Low: down, downstairs, in the dirt.

7. High: too tall, up, upstairs.

8. Combinations: high and tight, high and in, high and inside, up and in, up and inside, low and in, low and inside, down and in, down and inside, high and away, up and away, low and away, down and away, down and out, high and wide, high and outside, low and wide, low and outside.

"Juuuuuuuuuust... a bit outside."
– broadcaster Harry Doyle, *Major League* (1989)

swing
n. cut, hack, riffle, rip, whack
v. accept, attempt, buggywhip, chase, cut, go after, hack, lash, offer, pull the trigger, rip, take a whack; SPANISH abanicar

• A batter who swings as hard as he can is "going for the downs," "letting it rip," "swinging for the fences," or "swinging from his heels."

• swing and miss
v. bite, come up empty, fail, fan, fish, get baited, pull a Casey, send up a breeze, swing through, whiff

• let a pitch pass without swinging
v. admire, appraise, consider, contemplate, disregard, examine, eye, eyeball, hold back, ignore, inspect, lay off, let pass, look at, look over, observe, regard, scrutinize, study, survey, take, watch

• A batter given the signal to "swing away" by his third-base coach receives the "green light." A batter given the signal to "take" by his third-base coach receives the "red light."

"Gentlemen, swinging the bat is a great exercise. It strengthens the diaphragm and loosens pent-up emotions in the chest. Besides, you may hit the ball."
– Hall of Fame manager Billy Southworth (1929, 1940-1951), to his Cardinals before Game 3 of the 1944 World Series, quoted by writer John P. Carmichael

switch-hitter
n. batter from both sides, switch-sticker, turn-around hitter, turn-over hitter; SPANISH bateador ambidestro

• A switch-hitter is a batter who is able to hit from either side of the plate, hitting left-handed against right-handed pitchers and right-handed against left-handers.

• Pat Venditte is the only current switch-pitcher in professional baseball, able to pitch with either his left or his right arm. Other switch-pitchers include Greg A. Harris (1981-1995, though only specifically on September 28, 1995 in the majors) and 19th century switch-hurlers Larry Corcoran, Elton Chamberlain, and "The Apollo of the Box," Tony Mullane.

• Corcoran was noteworthy for more than just switch-pitching. He was one of the very first pitchers to signal in advance to his catcher which pitch he was throwing, moving his tobacco from side to side in his mouth as an indicator.

• Mullane was good-looking (hence his nickname) and talented, but did not do himself any favors with his treatment of African-American pioneer Moses Fleetwood "Fleet" Walker in 1884, whom he attempted to injure with stray pitches while ignoring the catcher's signs. It is very likely, too, that the majority of his switch-pitching occurred in exhibition games.

T

Christy Mathewson and Walter Johnson.
(Courtesy Library of Congress, LC-DIG-hec-01442

team

n. bunch, club, group, men, nine, outfit, squad, troop, troupe, unit; SPANISH equipo

"Baseball is a team game, but it is played by individuals who do their job singly and alone, in the full glare of the spotlight. They will be praised or blamed, become heroes or goats, depending on their performance under pressure."
– Lawrence Ritter, *The Story of Baseball*

third base

n. coffin corner, corner, difficult corner, difficult station, far corner, far turn, hot corner, third, third sack; SPANISH antesala, tercera base

throw

n. chuck, dealing, delivery, feed, flip, heave, lob, offering, peg, pitch, relay, shovel, sling, toss; SPANISH tiro
v. bring, buggywhip, cast, catapult, chuck, crank, deal, deliver, direct, dish, distribute, face, feed, fire, fling, flip, go, guide, gun, heave, hurl, jump throw, launch, let fly, lob, loose, offer, peg, pitch, present, propel, push, relay, release, rifle, roll, sidearm, serve, shotput, shovel, sling, spin, steer, toss, transfer, transport, twirl, unleash, whip, wing; SPANISH tirar

• A player with a strong arm is said to have a bazooka, cannon, gun, hose, howitzer, rifle, or shotgun.

• throw poorly

v. airmail, banana, bounce, hop, miss, overshoot, overthrow, sail, shortarm, skip, spray, uncork

• An inaccurate throwing arm is considered "buckshot," a

"scatter arm," or "scattershot."

• A fielder who hesitates in mid throwing motion before rearing back once more and firing is said to have "double-clutched" or "double-pumped."

• A fielder who throws a "parachute" to first base puts too much air under the ball, allowing the runner to beat the throw.

• On May 20, 1956, Bruce Nash and Allan Zullo noted in *The Baseball Hall of Shame 2*, Washington Senators pitcher "Chuck Stobbs uncorked the wildest pitch in Major League history. It was a "tape-measure" throw that sailed 30 feet toward the first base side of home plate – and landed 17 rows up in the stands! … "I was so surprised," recalled Stobbs, who lost the game 4-2. 'I didn't know if I should dig a hole and try to hide under the mound…. All I could do was stand there and wait for the umpire to throw me a new ball.' "

trade
n. bargain, deal, exchange, swap, transaction
v. deal, dispatch, exchange, flip, flip-flop, peddle, send, ship, swap, switch; SPANISH cambio

• A team looking to trade a player is said to "put him on the market," "put him on the block," or "shop him around."

• A "challenge trade" sees two players of the same position traded for one another, pitting the players against one another in direct comparison and making it easy to see which team received the better end of the trade afterward.

• A trade is often described in terms of the quantity of

players involved. For instance, a trade that sees a team trade three players and receive one player in return can be described as either a "four-player deal" or a "three-for-one."

• A "fire sale" sees a team trade off all of its top players at once, "breaking up the team."

• A trade that clearly favors one team over the other is a cheat, fleecing, rip-off, robbery (or highway robbery), scam, steal, swindle, theft, and may very well have seen one team sell the other a "bill of goods."

"Getting traded was like being sent to a different family on Christmas morning."

– Ed Lynch (1980-1987)

triple

n. three-bagger, three-base hit, three-baser, three-master, three-sacker, triple bag, triple bagger, triple baser, triplet; SPANISH tribey, triple

• Legend has it that Boston's Fenway Park presents the potential for a ground-rule triple. A mesh net used to hang at the top of the Green Monster, the ballpark's famous left-field wall, collecting home-run balls. A Red Sox employee later retrieved the baseballs by climbing a ladder attached to the wall. Before the 2003 season, an enormously popular seating section (the "Monster seats") replaced the net. The ladder remains, a reminder of seasons past. If a fly ball lodges in the ladder, the legend has it, a ground-rule triple is awarded to the batter. It's a great story, passed along freely by Fenway faithful, but unsubstantiated in the official ground rules of the ballpark.

• High triples totals have fallen as the decades have passed by and ballparks with closer walls and smaller power alleys have come into fashion. Detroit Tigers Hall of Famer Sam Crawford (1899-1917) holds the career record with 309 triples in his sterling career.

• The single-season triples record is owned by John "Chief" Wilson (1908-1916), who piled up 36 three-baggers in 1912, nearly three times his highest total in any other season.

triple play
n. three-ply killing, triple killing, triplet

• A triple play requires a situation of at least two runners on the bases and no outs in order to even present the possibility of taking place, making it one of the rarer diamond feats. Still, at Fenway Park on July 17, 1990, the Boston Red Sox hit into a pair of triple plays against the Minnesota Twins, the first time in Major League history in which two triple plays occurred in the same game. "Well," said Sox pitcher Dennis Lamp, "we did keep out of the double play." The very next day, the two teams combined to hit into a Major League record 10 double plays.

• Pitcher Ken Ash (1925, 1928-1930) had a career won-lost record of just 6-8, but the sixth win came in abruptly triumphant fashion. On July 27, 1930, Ash came out of the Cincinnati Reds bullpen to face a threatening Cubs offense. He tossed only one pitch, coaxing an inning-ending triple play from Charlie "Jolly Cholly" Grimm. The Reds won the game, 6-5, handing Ash the final victory of his career.

• Joe Pignatano (1956-1962) suffered the opposite fate of Ash. A member for the woefully miserable expansion New

York Mets of 1962, a team that finished with a 40-120 record, Pignatano lined into a triple play to end the eighth inning on the final day of the 1962 season. It was his only at-bat of the game, and the last at-bat of his career.

• If a triple play is rare, an unassisted triple play, with all three outs recorded by the same fielder, is extraordinary. From 1900 to 2011, there were only 15 unassisted triple plays in the Major Leagues, all performed by a first baseman, second baseman, or shortstop. The Cubs' Jimmy Cooney and the Tigers' Johnny Neun performed unassisted triple plays on consecutive days, May 30 and May 31, 1927. Over the next 65 years, the Major Leagues would experience only one unassisted triple play, turned by the Senators' Ron Hansen on July 30, 1968. Things have heated up recently, though. Philadelphia Phillies second baseman Eric Bruntlett turned a game-ending unassisted triple play against the New York Mets on August 23, 2009, marking the fourth time in 10 years that an unassisted triple play was performed.

• There has only been one triple play in World Series history. It was recorded in unassisted fashion by Cleveland second baseman Bill Wambsganss in Game 5 of the 1920 Series against Brooklyn.

U

Roger Peckinpaugh, New York, AL (left), and Dave Bancroft, New York, NL (right), with umpires at Polo Grounds, World Series, 1921.
(Courtesy Library of Congress, LC-DIG-ggbain-33189.)

umpire
n. arbiter, arbitrator, judge, justice, masked man (if home plate umpire); INSULTING blind tom, blue, bluecoat, boy blue, boy in blue, dog robber, Jesse James, man in blue, Mr. Guess, robber, sheepherder, tin cup, ump; SPANISH árbitro

• An umpire "calls 'em as he sees 'em."

" 'Play!' I said. (Contrary to popular myth, umpires don't say, 'Play ball!' Why everyone thinks they do, I don't know.)"

– Bruce Weber, *As They See 'Em*

"Ideally, the umpire should combine the integrity of a Supreme Court justice, the physical agility of an acrobat, the endurance of Job and the imperturbability of Buddha."

– *Time* magazine; August 25, 1961

• complain about an umpire's call
v. air grievances, beef, bellyache, carp, cavil, chaff, chew out, chirp, contravene, criticize, denounce, differ, disagree, disapprove, dispute, dissent, fuss, gripe, groan, grouse, growl, grumble, lament, make a fuss, moan, nag, object, oppose, protest, rebut, refute, ride, sound off, squawk, whine

• It is considered permissible for managers and players to dispute a call as long as they are brief and don't "show up" the umpire. An umpire's strike zone tends to be another touchy subject – arguing balls and strikes is an easy way to receive an ejection.

• declare a called strike three
v. call out, punch out, ring up

• eject from a game
v. banish, bid farewell, boot, bounce, dismiss, disqualify, exile, expel, evict, get rid of, give the gate, give the thumb, give the heave-ho, oust, send to the showers, show the door, throw out, thumb, toss, toss out

• An ejection is often precipitated by "saying the magic word(s)."

uniform

n. apparel, appearance, attire, colors, costume, dress, duds, garb, garments, gear, getup, jersey, livery, look, outfit, regalia, suit, threads, uni, vestment, wardrobe; SPECIFIC alternate jersey, home jersey, home whites, pinstripes, road grays, road jersey, Sunday jersey, third jersey

• A baseball uniform consists of spikes (shoes, never called cleats), stirrups or socks (often pulled up to just below the knee), jersey pants, a belt, double-knit jersey tops, and a baseball cap to top it off.

• Baseball teams began wearing white jerseys at home and gray jerseys on the road because it was easier to do laundry at home than on the road.

• An "alternate" or "third jersey" is worn in addition to a team's usual home and road uniforms. If the jersey is only worn on Sundays, it's considered a "Sunday jersey."

• It is mandated that managers and coaches wear the same uniforms as their players, though manager Burt Shotten (Philadelphia, 1928-1933; Cincinnati, 1934; Brooklyn, 1947-1950) and Philadelphia's Hall of Fame owner/manager Connie Mack each eschewed uniforms in favor of dapper suits during games.

• The original baseball uniforms worn by the Knickerbocker Base Ball Club in 1849 comprised collared flannel shirts and woolen pantaloons. Nineteen years later, the Cincinnati Red Stockings substituted knickers for pantaloons.

• On August 8, 1976, the White Sox suited up in ill-advised

Bermuda shorts for Game 1 of a doubleheader against the Kansas City Royals. The style choice was the idea of owner Bill Veeck; safe to say it wasn't one of Veeck's more popular innovations. The Sox won, 5-2, then changed into their usual jersey pants between games, packing the shorts away for good. The White Sox weren't the first team to try out shorts for a game, though; that distinction belongs to the 1950 Hollywood Stars of the Pacific Coast League.

• The National League came up with the original – and short-lived – idea in 1882 to color-code each defensive position, thereby easing the education for new fans of the game. As Bruce Nash and Allan Zullo detail in *The Baseball Hall of Shame*, "White was the compulsory color for all pants, belts and ties. But the jerseys came in various combinations, depending on the position:

> Pitcher, light blue;
> Catcher, scarlet;
> First baseman, scarlet and white;
> Second baseman, orange and black;
> Third baseman, gray and white;
> Shortstop, maroon;
> Left fielder, white;
> Center fielder, red and black;
> Right fielder, gray;
> Substitute, green; and another substitute, brown."

• The Atlantic League's Reading Red Roses first tried out numbers on their uniforms in 1907, an innovation that had to wait until the 1916 Cleveland Indians to be introduced in the Major Leagues. The 1960 Chicago White Sox were the first teams to place player surnames on the backs of jerseys.

• The first uniform number retired (preventing any subsequent player from wearing the number) in the Major

Leagues was #4 for the New York Yankees, worn by Hall of Fame first baseman Lou Gehrig (1923-1939). The number was retired in a special ceremony on July 4, 1939, Lou Gehrig Appreciation Day at Yankee Stadium.

• On April 15, 1997, Major League Baseball retired #42 in honor of Hall of Fame second baseman Jackie Robinson (1947-1956), the 50th anniversary of the day Robinson broke the Major League color barrier.

"You wouldn't believe the players' off-field clothes. Now I know why the league insists that they wear uniforms."

– Ken Levine

Fans lining up for World Series bleacher seats at Yankee Stadium.
(Courtesy Library of Congress, LC-DIG-ggbain-36450

walk
n. Annie Oakley, base on balls, BB, casualty pass, four wide ones, free check, free pass, free passage, free ride, free ticket, free transit, furlough, gift, handout, life, pass, passport, phantom hit, promenade, ticket to first; SPANISH caminata, base por bola, pasaporte

• **receive a walk**
v. achieve, attain, coax, deadhead, draw, earn, get issued, obtain, wait out, work, wrangle

• According to Paul Dickson in his *Dickson Baseball*

Dictionary, here is the origin of the term "Annie Oakley" carrying the most credibility: A walk is also known as a free pass, and a free pass to a baseball game (that is, a free ticket) was signified in the early days of the twentieth century by having holes punched in it. A "baseball magnate," perhaps American League Commissioner Ban Johnson, looked at such a ticket and commented that it looked much like the playing cards Annie Oakley famously shot holes through in her well-known act.

• An intentional walk incorporates "four free wide ones" and "takes the bat out of the hitter's hands." Hall of Famer Willie McCovey (1959-1980) owned the Major League record for most intentional walks with 45, set in 1969, but that standard was shattered by Barry Bonds (1986-2007). In 2002, Bonds was intentionally passed 68 times. In 2004, the mark shot up to an astonishing 120 intentional walks, part of Bonds' Major League record 232 walks for the season. The left fielder compiled a record-breaking 2,558 walks in his 22 seasons in the Majors.

• Babe Ruth piled up walks via the intimidating threat of the home run, Ted Williams via an extraordinary batter's eye, and Barry Bonds via a combination of the two. Then there was Eddie Yost (1944, 1946-1962), a 5'10" leadoff hitter for the Washington Senators before finishing his career with the Detroit Tigers and Los Angeles Angels. Yost was nicknamed "The Walking Man," a moniker he earned by leading the American League in walks in six different seasons. The New York University product topping 120 walks in eight different seasons and finished his career with 1,614 walks compared to just 920 strikeouts.

wall

n. see *outfield wall*

win
n. success, triumph, victory, W; SPANISH ganado
v. overcome, succeed, triumph; see "defeat;" SPANISH ganar

• The pitcher who receives a win or a loss from a game's outcome receives a "decision."

• A team on a winning streak is ascending, blazing, catching fire, charging, clicking, climbing (the standings), coming together, cooking, flowing, flying, gelling, hard-charging, hitting on all cylinders, hot, humming, on fire, on a roll, rallying, rising, rolling, soaring, sizzling, streaking, surging, or taking off.

• The longest winning streak in Major League history belongs to the 1916 New York Giants, who reeled off 26 victories (and one tie) between September 7 and September 30. Even so, the 86-66 Giants finished fourth in the eight-team National League. First went to the 94-60 Brooklyn Robins, who were then trounced in the World Series by the American League champion Boston Red Sox.

• **receive the victory, as a pitcher**
v. achieve, attain, capture, collect, earn, gain, garner, get, land, merit, notch, obtain, pick up, reap, receive, score, secure, snag, snatch, take, vultch, vulture; SPANISH ganar

• See *relief pitcher* for "vulture" explanation.

World Series
n. Autumn Classic, Big Classic, Big Dance, Classic, Fall

Classic, promised land, the Series, World Serious (in jest); SPANISH serie mundial

• In the early part of the 1880s, two professional baseball leagues first pitted their champions against one another in a series to determine the best team of the nation. The National League was the (relatively young) establishment, founded in 1876. The American Association felt it had a stake for equality and scheduled its champion against the NL winner each year until the leagues merged under the National League name in 1891.

• The upstart American League began operations in 1901as a direct threat to the National League. In 1903, the first World Series (originally called the "World's Championship Series" and later the "World's Series") was held AL champ Boston against NL title bearer Pittsburgh. The upstarts mustered up the upset, bringing pride to the junior circuit.

• There was no championship series between the two leagues in 1904 due to the decision of the arrogant National League-winning New York Giants. Manager John McGraw had announced in late July, "The Giants will not play a postseason series with the American League champions. [AL President] Ban Johnson has not been on the level with me personally, and the American League management has been crooked more than once." McGraw's mind changed the next year. The men of Gotham repeated as NL champs in 1905 and consented to face the American League's Philadelphia Athletics (whom they defeated in five close games). It would take another 90 seasons before the next World Series was skipped, occurring due to the players' strike of 1994.

Bibliography

http://www.baseball-almanac.com/
http://www.baseball-reference.com/

Benson, Robert. *The Game: One Man, Nine Innings, A Love Affair with Baseball.* New York: Tarcher, 2001.

Dickson, Paul. *Baseball's Greatest Quotations, Revised Edition*. New York: HarperCollins Publishers, 2008.

Dickson, Paul, and McAfee, Skip. *The Dickson Baseball Dictionary*. New York: Avon Books, 1989.

Dickson, Paul, and McAfee, Skip. *The NEW Dickson Baseball Dictionary*. New York: Mariner Books, 1999.

Dickson, Paul, and McAfee, Skip. *The Dickson Baseball Dictionary, Third Edition*. New York: W.W. Norton & Company, Inc., 2009.

Dickson, Paul. *The Unwritten Rules of Baseball*. New York: HarperCollins Publishers, 2009.

Dravecky, Dave, with Tim Stafford. *Comeback*. Grand Rapids, Mich.: Zondervan, 1990.

"Dressed to the Nines, A History of the Baseball Uniform." Baseball Hall of Fame. http://exhibits.baseballhalloffame.org/dressed_to_the_nines

Garagiola, Joe. *It's Anybody's Ballgame*. Chicago: Contemporary Books, 1988.

Hample, Zack. *Watching Baseball Smarter.* New York: Vintage Books, 2007.

Handrinos, Peter. *The Funniest Baseball Book Ever*. Kansas City: Andrews McMeel Publishing, LLC, 2010.

James, Bill. *The New Bill James Historical Baseball Abstract*. New York: Free Press, 2001.

Lane, F.C. *Batting*. Lincoln, Nebraska: University of Nebraska Press, 2001.

Leventhal, Josh. *Take Me Out to the Ballpark.* New York: Black Dog & Leventhal Publishers, Inc., 2000.

Levine, Ken. *It's Gone! ... No, Wait a Minute....* New York: Villard Books, 1993.

Lewin, Esther, and Lewin, Albert E. *The Thesaurus of Slang*. New York: Facts on File, Inc., 1994.

Mazer, Bill. *Bill Mazer's Amazin' Baseball Book*. New York: Kensington Publishing Corps., 1990.

McCarthy, Matt. *Odd Man Out*. New York: Viking, 2009.

Morris, Peter. *A Game of Inches*. Chicago: Ivan R. Dee, 2006.

Murphy, Cait. *Crazy '08*. New York: HarperCollins Publishers Inc., 2007.

Nash, Bruce, and Zullo, Allan. *The Baseball Hall of Shame*. New York: Pocket Books, 1985.

Nash, Bruce, and Zullo, Allan. *The Baseball Hall of Shame 2*. New York: Pocket Books, 1986.

Nash, Bruce, and Zullo, Allan. *The Baseball Hall of Shame 3*. New York: Pocket Books, 1987.

Nash, Bruce, and Zullo, Allan. *The Baseball Hall of Shame's Warped Record Book*. New York: Collier Books, 1991.

Neyer, Rob, and James, Bill. *The Neyer/James Guide to Pitchers*. New York: Fireside, 2004.

Okrent, Daniel, and Wulf, Steve. *Baseball Anecdotes*. New York: Oxford University Press, 1989.

Pahigian, Josh. *The Seventh Inning Stretch*. Connecticut: Lyons Press, 2010.

Peterson, Robert. *Only the Ball was White*. New York: Oxford University Press, 1970.

Princeton Language Institute. *Roget's 21st Century Thesaurus.* New York: Bantam Dell, 2005.

Sansavere, Bob (June 23, 2011). "Twins giving of their per diem." *St. Paul Pioneer Press.*

Schlossberg, Dan. *Baseball Gold.* Chicago: Triumph Books, 2007.

Sheinin, Dave (April 18, 2006). "Long memories from a baseball classic." *Washington Post.*

Weber, Bruce. *As They See 'Em.* New York: Scribner, 2009.

Will, George. *Men at Work.* New York: Macmillan Publishing Company, 1990.

ABOUT THE AUTHOR

A native of Greenbelt, Maryland, Jesse Goldberg-Strassler graduated from Ithaca College in 2004. After broadcasting for the back-to-back Southern League Champion Montgomery Biscuits in 2006-2007, he joined the Frontier League Champion Windy City ThunderBolts in 2008 and was named a Runner-Up for Ballpark Digest's Broadcaster of the Year. Jesse currently serves as the Voice of the Lansing Lugnuts and writes about baseball for BallparkDigest.com.